Recursion's Revelations

Recursive Algorithm Design, Implementation, and Applications in Programming

Evelyn Blackwell

Contents

1 Introduction to Recursion

Recursion, at its core, is a powerful programming paradigm where a function calls itself. This self-referential nature allows us to elegantly solve problems that can be broken down into smaller, self-similar subproblems. Imagine a set of Russian nesting dolls; each doll contains a smaller version of itself, until you reach the smallest doll. Recursion works similarly, tackling a problem by repeatedly breaking it down until a simple, solvable base case is reached. This base case is crucial; without it, the function would call itself infinitely, leading to a stack overflow error, a common pitfall for beginning programmers. Understanding this fundamental principle is the first step towards mastering recursion.

The key to successfully implementing recursive functions lies in identifying the base case and the recursive step. The base case is the simplest version of the problem, the one that can be solved directly without further recursion. For example, in calculating a factorial, the base case is when the number is 0 or 1, as their factorials are defined as 1. The recursive step defines how the problem is broken down into smaller subproblems and how their solutions are combined to solve the original problem. For the factorial, the recursive step involves multiplying the current number by the factorial of the number minus one. Careful consideration of both components is vital for correct and efficient recursive algorithms.

Consider the classic example of the Fibonacci sequence: each number is the sum of the two preceding ones. This inherently recursive definition lends itself perfectly to a recursive solution. However, a naive recursive implementation can be incredibly inefficient for larger numbers, due to redundant calculations. We'll explore optimization techniques later, but for now, understand the core principle: define your base case (usually the first one or two Fibonacci numbers), and then recursively calculate subsequent numbers based on the sum of the preceding two. This demonstrates the elegance of recursion, but also highlights the importance of considering efficiency.

Let's delve into the practical aspects of designing recursive algorithms. Begin by carefully analyzing the problem. Can it be broken down into smaller, self-similar subproblems? If so, identify the base case – the simplest instance of the problem that can be solved without recursion. Then, work on the recursive step – the part that reduces the problem to a smaller instance and combines the solution of the smaller instance with other parts to create the solution for the main problem. This systematic approach is essential, making sure your design is clear and helps prevent the common pitfalls of recursion.

Many data structures are inherently recursive. Consider a tree; each node can be viewed as a smaller tree itself. This recursive nature makes recursive algorithms ideal for tasks like tree traversal. Imagine traversing a directory structure on your computer. You start at the root directory, and for each subdirectory, you perform the same process recursively until you reach the files. This is analogous to how recursive functions explore tree structures, navigating from the root node to its children, and their children, and so on, until it reaches the leaves. This is a powerful example illustrating recursion's natural connection to several common data structures.

Mastering recursion requires practice and patience. Start with simple problems, carefully consider the base case and recursive step, and test your solution thoroughly. Don't be discouraged by initial difficulties; recursion is a powerful tool once mastered. By working through examples and systematically applying the design principles outlined, you'll gain confidence and proficiency. It's a journey of understanding; embracing the iterative process of learning, refinement, and adaptation will be crucial to your overall success. Remember the power of recursion lies in its ability to elegantly express inherently self-similar problems, making complex tasks manageable and understandable.

1.1 What is Recursion?

Recursion, at its core, is a powerful programming technique where a function calls itself within its own definition. Imagine a set of Russian nesting dolls: each doll contains a smaller version of itself, until you reach the smallest doll. Recursion works similarly; a problem is broken down into smaller, self-similar subproblems, each solved by the same function, until a simple, easily solvable base case is reached. This base case prevents the function from calling itself infinitely, ensuring the process eventually terminates. Without a base case, recursion becomes an endless loop, mirroring the impossible task of finding the smallest doll inside an infinite set of nesting dolls.

Understanding recursion requires a shift in thinking. It's not about tracing the execution step-by-step, which can quickly become overwhelming. Instead, focus on the overall structure: how the problem is divided, how the subproblems are solved, and how the results are combined. Think of it like understanding a fractal pattern; you don't need to meticulously draw every tiny detail, but grasping the self-similarity of the pattern reveals the whole. This abstract understanding is key to writing effective recursive code. You will gain a deeper appreciation for the elegance and power of this approach as you become more familiar with its applications.

Let's illustrate with a simple example: calculating the factorial of a number. The factorial of a non-negative integer n (denoted as n!) is the product of all positive integers less than or equal to n. For instance, 5! = 5 \emph{ 4 } 3 \emph{ 2 } 1 = 120. Recursively, we can define n! as n * (n-1)!, where 0! is defined as 1 (this is our base case). The function calls itself to calculate the factorial of a smaller number until it reaches the base case of 0!, at which point the recursion unwinds, multiplying the results back up to obtain the final answer. This approach mirrors the nested structure of a mathematical definition where the factorial of a number is expressed in terms of the factorial of a smaller number, a perfect example of self-similarity.

The beauty of recursion lies in its ability to elegantly solve problems with inherent recursive structures. Consider traversing a tree data structure. A tree, by definition, consists of nodes, each possibly having children that are themselves smaller trees. To traverse the tree, you visit a node, then recursively traverse its children. This process mirrors the recursive structure of the tree, making the solution both intuitive and concise. This efficient traversal allows for powerful operations on tree structures without the added complexity of iterative approaches. Note that this simplicity does not necessarily translate to efficient runtime in all cases, so it is important to analyze the problem context.

However, recursion isn't always the optimal solution. Excessive recursion can lead to stack overflow errors, where the program runs out of memory to store the function calls. This is because each recursive call adds a new frame to the call stack, a data structure that keeps track of function calls. If the recursion goes too deep, the stack overflows. Deep recursion might prove inefficient on large datasets. Therefore, programmers must carefully consider whether recursion is the most appropriate solution for a given problem, considering the depth and breadth of the recursion tree. Carefully assessing your problem structure can significantly improve your selection between recursive and iterative approaches. This is where understanding the problem's properties is paramount.

Moreover, the elegance of recursion can sometimes mask its computa-

tional cost. Recursive solutions can be less efficient than iterative ones, especially for problems that don't have a naturally recursive structure. For example, while you can write a recursive algorithm for finding the sum of numbers in an array, an iterative approach is often simpler and more efficient. The overhead of function calls in recursion can accumulate, leading to a performance bottleneck. Careful analysis of the algorithm's time and space complexity is crucial before implementing a recursive solution.
Ultimately, the decision of whether or not to use recursion depends on the specific problem and context. While it provides elegance and conciseness for problems with naturally recursive structures, its potential for stack overflow and inefficiencies must be carefully considered. A deep understanding of recursion's strengths and weaknesses allows programmers to leverage its power effectively and make informed decisions about when to use this powerful technique. As you progress in your understanding, you will appreciate when and how to apply these concepts. Understanding both the theoretical underpinnings and practical implications of recursive solutions is crucial for developing robust and efficient programs.

1.2 Recursive Thinking

Recursive thinking isn't about magically conjuring solutions; it's a structured approach to problem-solving. Imagine you're facing a complex task, like organizing a massive library. Instead of tackling the entire library at once, a recursive thinker would focus on a smaller, self-similar unit—a single shelf, perhaps. They'd organize that shelf, then apply the same method to the next shelf, and the next, until the whole library is meticulously arranged. This is the essence of recursion: breaking a large problem into identical smaller problems, solving those, and combining the results. The key is identifying this self-similarity—the pattern that repeats at different scales. This pattern recognition is the core skill of effective recursive problem-solving.

The beauty of recursion lies in its elegance and conciseness. A single, well-defined recursive function can elegantly handle vast amounts of data or complex operations, often replacing lengthy iterative loops. Consider calculating the factorial of a number. An iterative approach might involve a loop, incrementally multiplying numbers. A recursive approach, however, defines the factorial of a number as the number multiplied by the factorial of the number minus one, until you reach the base case (factorial of 0 is 1). This recursive definition mirrors the problem's inherent structure, leading to far more compact and readable code. It's a testament to the power of leveraging inherent problem structure. Understanding this structure is critical to apply recursive thinking effectively.

However, the apparent simplicity hides potential pitfalls. The most common is infinite recursion, akin to an infinitely nested set of Russian dolls. Without a clearly defined base case – a condition that stops the recursive calls – the function will call itself endlessly, ultimately crashing your program. This emphasizes the importance of meticulous planning. Define your base case explicitly; it's the anchor that prevents your recursion from spiraling into oblivion. Think of it as the ground floor of your recursive building; without it, the whole structure collapses. Always start with the base case; it's your foundation.

Let's consider another scenario: traversing a tree data structure. A tree, by its very nature, exhibits recursive properties. Each node in a tree can be viewed as a smaller tree itself. To traverse the entire tree, you can recursively visit each node, processing its data and then recursively traversing its children (sub-trees). This approach beautifully mirrors the tree's hierarchical structure. It's both intuitive and efficient. The recursive algorithm neatly mirrors the data structure's recursive definition; this synergy is a hallmark of effective recursive solutions.

Identifying suitable problems for recursive solutions is crucial. Not all problems are amenable to a recursive approach. Problems that exhibit self-similarity—where the solution to the overall problem can be constructed from the solutions to smaller, self-similar subproblems—are prime candidates. If you can break down a problem into smaller, identical instances, you've found a strong hint that recursion might be the right tool for the job. The clearer you understand the problem, the easier it will be to spot the recursive structure. Remember, not every problem needs a recursive solution; choose your tools wisely.

In addition to its elegance, recursion can offer performance advantages. Recursive algorithms are often remarkably efficient when implemented correctly. However, this efficiency is conditional. Poorly designed recursive solutions can easily lead to excessive overhead and stack overflow. Therefore, optimization is vital. Techniques such as memoization (caching previously computed results) and tail recursion optimization (a technique to minimize stack usage) can dramatically improve recursive algorithm performance. These enhancements can make recursive algorithms perform comparably to or even better than their iterative counterparts, if not better.

Finally, recursive thinking transcends the confines of programming. It's a valuable problem-solving technique applicable across various domains. From planning complex projects to tackling challenging puzzles, breaking down large problems into smaller, manageable pieces—a core principle of recursion—is often a key to success. The iterative application of smaller, simpler processes yields a large-scale, complex result; recursive thinking makes this iterative application manageable and understandable. Practice recursive thinking, and you will find that your analytical skills improve. Learning recursion is not just about learning a programming technique; it's about developing a different way of approaching problems.

2 Basic Recursive Techniques

The factorial function, a staple in introductory programming, provides a perfect illustration of recursion's elegance. Calculating 5! (5 factorial) isn't just 5 \emph{ 4 } 3 \emph{ 2 } 1; it's also 5 \emph{ 4!. See the pattern? We can define 5! recursively as 5 multiplied by the factorial of the number immediately preceding it. This self-referential definition is the heart of recursive programming. A recursive function calls itself, chipping away at the problem until a simple, solvable base case is reached. In this case, the base case is 0!, which is defined as 1. Without a base case, our function would call itself endlessly, resulting in a dreaded stack overflow error – a crucial concept to understand and avoid. The recursive implementation might look like this: function factorial(n) { if (n === 0) return 1; else return n } factorial(n \item 1); }. This concise code encapsulates the entire logic, showcasing the power and brevity often associated with recursive solutions. The beauty lies in its simplicity – a single function elegantly handles the calculation, avoiding the need for iterative loops or complex iterative logic. Learning to recognize this pattern of self-similarity is key to mastering recursive problem-solving.

Next, let's tackle the Fibonacci sequence, a classic example showcasing recursion's versatility. This sequence, where each number is the sum of the two preceding ones (0, 1, 1, 2, 3, 5, and so on), elegantly lends itself to a recursive implementation. Each Fibonacci number is recursively defined in terms of the two numbers before it. However, a naive recursive imple-

mentation of the Fibonacci sequence can be incredibly inefficient, suffering from repeated calculations. This inefficiency stems from recalculating the same Fibonacci numbers multiple times within the recursive calls. For example, calculating F(5) requires calculating F(4) and F(3). Calculating F(4) requires F(3) and F(2), and F(3) is calculated again. This redundant computation leads to exponential time complexity, making it unsuitable for larger values of n. To illustrate the point: function fibonacci(n) { if (n <= 1) return n; else return fibonacci(n \item 1) + fibonacci(n - 2); }. While simple, this approach quickly becomes computationally expensive as n grows. Consider the Tower of Hanoi, a classic puzzle that beautifully demonstrates recursion's problem-solving power. In this puzzle, you have three rods and a set of disks of different sizes, stacked in decreasing order of size on one rod. The goal is to move the entire stack to another rod, one disk at a time, adhering to two rules: only one disk can be moved at a time, and a larger disk can never be placed on top of a smaller disk. The recursive solution cleverly breaks down the problem into smaller, self-similar subproblems. To move n disks from source rod A to destination rod C, you can: 1) Recursively move n-1 disks from A to the auxiliary rod B; 2) Move the largest disk (nth disk) from A to C; 3) Recursively move the n-1 disks from B to C. The base case is when n = 1 (only one disk), where the solution is trivial: just move the single disk to the destination rod. This approach mirrors the recursive structure of the problem, elegantly expressing the solution in a concise and understandable manner. The recursive solution's structure perfectly matches the problem's inherent self-similarity, making it an excellent example of the power and elegance of recursive thinking. It's a fantastic exercise in visualizing the recursive process, understanding how the smaller subproblems contribute to solving the larger problem, and seeing the recursive function call itself until it reaches the base case.
These three examples – factorial calculation, Fibonacci sequence generation, and the Tower of Hanoi puzzle – serve as foundational stepping

stones. They illustrate core recursive patterns: identifying the base case, defining the recursive step, and understanding how the recursive calls unravel to solve the problem. Mastering these examples unlocks the door to tackling more complex recursive problems, solidifying your understanding of this powerful programming paradigm. Remember, the key lies in recognizing the inherent self-similarity within a problem and translating that self-similarity into a recursive function that elegantly breaks down the problem into smaller, manageable parts. While challenges may arise, the rewards of elegant and efficient code will be worth the effort. Keep practicing, and the recursive approach will become increasingly intuitive and effective. By understanding these basics, you will lay a solid groundwork for exploring more advanced recursive techniques and applying them to increasingly sophisticated programming challenges.

2.1 Factorial Calculation

The factorial of a non-negative integer n, denoted as n!, is the product of all positive integers less than or equal to n. For example, $5! = 5 \times 4 \times 3 \times 2 \times 1 = 120$. This seemingly simple calculation provides a perfect illustration of recursion's elegance and power. Understanding its recursive implementation is crucial for grasping the fundamental concepts behind recursive algorithms.

A recursive approach to calculating factorials elegantly mirrors the mathematical definition. We can define the factorial of n as n multiplied by the factorial of n-1. This self-referential definition forms the heart of our recursive function. The key, however, lies in establishing a base case. This base case prevents the function from calling itself infinitely, a common pitfall in recursive programming. For factorials, the base case is when n equals 0; the factorial of 0 is defined as 1.

Let's examine a simple C++ implementation:

cpp

```
int factorial(int n) {
if (n == 0) {
return 1; // Base case
} else {
return n * factorial(n \item 1); // Recursive step
}
}
```

This concise function perfectly captures the recursive definition. If n is 0, it immediately returns 1. Otherwise, it recursively calls itself with a smaller input (n-1), ultimately reaching the base case. The results of these recursive calls are then multiplied together, culminating in the correct factorial. Consider the execution for factorial(3): The initial call, factorial(3), returns 3 \emph{ factorial(2). factorial(2) then returns 2 } factorial(1), and factorial(1) returns 1 \emph{ factorial(0). Finally, factorial(0) hits the base case and returns 1. This value propagates back up the chain of calls: 1 } 1 = 1, 2 \emph{ 1 = 2, and 3 } 2 = 6, the correct factorial of 3.

It's important to visualize this step-by-step process. Each recursive call adds a new frame to the call stack. If the number is large, the stack could grow considerably. This illustrates the potential for stack overflow errors, a critical issue to address when dealing with recursion, especially for very large values of n. We'll explore techniques to mitigate this risk in a later chapter.

However, the recursive approach, while elegant, isn't always the most efficient. Iterative solutions often outperform recursive ones in terms of speed and memory usage, particularly for factorial calculations. An iterative solution avoids the overhead of function calls and stack management. Therefore, while the recursive implementation demonstrates the core concept beautifully, practical applications might favor iterative methods for better performance when dealing with large inputs. For beginners, it's valuable to understand both approaches and appreciate their tradeoffs.

Nevertheless, the elegance and conceptual clarity of the recursive approach remain invaluable in understanding recursive thinking and problem-solving. The factorial example serves as a building block. This basic understanding forms a solid foundation for tackling more complex recursive problems that can't easily be solved iteratively. Mastering this simple example unlocks the door to the power and versatility of recursive algorithms, paving the way for tackling far more challenging computational tasks. The recursive solution, although perhaps less efficient than its iterative counterpart in this specific case, provides a conceptual clarity and simplicity which is crucial for beginners to understand before moving on to more complex examples. This elegant solution emphasizes the beauty of recursive thinking. By mastering this seemingly simple task, you will gain a powerful tool for tackling more complex problems later in the book. Remember the importance of base cases; they are the bedrock of recursive programming, preventing infinite loops and ensuring correct results. The recursive approach, while not always the most performant, offers an insightful lens through which to view the problem and appreciate the power of self-referential functions. It's a stepping stone to more advanced concepts, and a solid understanding of this simple example will greatly assist in your journey to mastering recursion. The seemingly simple factorial function, therefore, acts as a microcosm of the broader power and potential complications inherent in recursive algorithm design.
The recursive implementation offers a clear and elegant representation of the mathematical definition, but remember to consider the potential for stack overflow errors and the relative performance compared to an iterative solution. Choosing the best approach depends on factors like the size of the input and the complexity of the problem. This chapter, however, primarily focuses on the conceptual understanding of recursive thinking using the familiar factorial calculation as a stepping stone to more intricate recursive concepts.

2.2 Fibonacci Sequence

The Fibonacci sequence, a seemingly simple series of numbers, holds a fascinating place in the world of recursive algorithms. Defined by the sum of the two preceding numbers, starting with 0 and 1, it elegantly illustrates the power and elegance of recursive thinking. We begin with 0 and 1; adding these gives us 1, then adding 1 and 1 results in 2, and subsequently, 2 + 1 = 3, 3 + 2 = 5, and so forth. The pattern, simple yet profound, creates a sequence of numbers that appear unexpectedly in various natural phenomena, from the branching of trees to the arrangement of petals on a flower.

Understanding how to implement this sequence recursively involves breaking down the problem into smaller, self-similar subproblems. The core idea is that any Fibonacci number can be defined in terms of the two numbers that precede it. Thus, to calculate the nth Fibonacci number, we need only calculate the (n-1)th and (n-2)th Fibonacci numbers and add them together. This forms the recursive step, the very heart of our algorithm. This recursive definition, however concise, requires careful handling of base cases.

These base cases are the crucial elements that prevent the algorithm from falling into an infinite loop, a common pitfall in recursive programming. Without them, the function would call itself endlessly, consuming ever-increasing amounts of memory and ultimately crashing the program. In the case of the Fibonacci sequence, the base cases are the first two numbers, F(0) = 0 and F(1) = 1. These provide the termination condition, the point at which the recursion stops and the final value is returned. Properly defining these base cases is not a trivial task; careful thought must be given to these initial conditions to ensure correctness and efficiency.

The practical implementation of this recursive approach involves writing a function that calls itself. This function takes an integer, n, representing the desired Fibonacci number as input. If n is 0 or 1, it returns the appropriate base case value. Otherwise, it recursively calls itself twice, once for (n-1) and once for (n-2), adds the results, and returns the sum. This simple, elegant solution, though efficient for smaller values of n, highlights a significant limitation of naive recursive approaches—exponential time complexity. Calculating larger Fibonacci numbers with this method rapidly becomes computationally expensive, leading to significant performance issues.

The inefficiency arises from redundant calculations. Consider calculating F(5). This requires calculating F(4) and F(3). Calculating F(4) in turn requires F(3) and F(2), and so on. Notice that F(3) is calculated multiple times, and this redundancy increases dramatically as n grows larger. This is a key point; we need to optimize the algorithm to avoid repeating calculations. Memoization, a technique discussed in detail in a later chapter, elegantly solves this problem by storing the results of previously computed Fibonacci numbers. With memoization, each computed value is stored in a data structure, usually a dictionary or an array, allowing for immediate retrieval instead of recalculating. This significantly improves the algorithm's efficiency, reducing the time complexity to linear.

Furthermore, consider the iterative approach to calculating the Fibonacci sequence. While conceptually simpler, it offers a powerful contrast to the recursive approach. This iterative solution employs a loop to sequentially calculate each Fibonacci number, building up the sequence step-by-step. It avoids the overhead of recursive function calls, making it generally more efficient than the straightforward recursive implementation. However, this iterative method lacks the inherent elegance and mathematical clarity displayed by the recursive solution; the recursive version directly mirrors the mathematical definition of the Fibonacci sequence.

Choosing between a recursive and iterative approach depends on the context. While the iterative approach offers superior performance for larger values of n, the recursive approach provides a more concise and arguably more intuitive representation of the mathematical problem. Understanding both approaches provides valuable insights into different programming paradigms and their respective trade-offs. The elegance of recursion in this particular example, however, is undeniably compelling. Its clarity allows for a deeper understanding of the problem's underlying structure and opens the door to exploring more complex recursive algorithms. This basic Fibonacci sequence, therefore, serves as a perfect foundational example to understand and later implement more sophisticated recursive techniques. This example lays the groundwork for our later exploration of dynamic programming and its application to more computationally intensive problems.

2.3 Tower of Hanoi

The Tower of Hanoi puzzle, a deceptively simple game with profound recursive implications, provides an excellent illustration of recursive problem-solving. Imagine three rods, A, B, and C, and a stack of differently sized disks on rod A, with the largest disk at the bottom. The goal is to move the entire stack of disks to rod C, adhering to two crucial rules: only one disk can be moved at a time, and a larger disk can never be placed on top of a smaller one.

This seemingly straightforward task presents a surprisingly complex challenge, especially as the number of disks increases. Trying to solve it intuitively, by moving disks haphazardly, quickly becomes overwhelming. However, the beauty of recursion lies in its ability to break this complex problem down into smaller, self-similar subproblems. We can achieve this by focusing on the movement of the largest disk. To move the largest disk from A to C, we first need to move the smaller n-1 disks from A to B, then move the largest disk to C, and finally, move the n-1 disks from B to C.

Notice the self-similarity? Moving the n-1 disks from A to B is the same problem as the original, just with one fewer disk. This recursive structure allows us to define a function that calls itself, with a smaller input each time. The base case, the stopping condition for the recursion, is when we have only one disk to move (n=1). In this instance, we simply move the disk directly from the source to the destination rod. Without this base case, the function would call itself infinitely, leading to a dreaded stack overflow error.

Let's consider a practical example using three disks. To move all three disks from A to C, we first recursively move the top two disks from A to B using the same algorithm. This involves moving the smallest disk from A to C, then the medium disk from A to B, and finally the smallest disk from C to B. Then, we move the largest disk from A to C. Finally, we recursively move the two disks from B to C, mirroring the steps we took to move them from A to B. The recursive solution elegantly handles this seemingly complex task. Understanding this process is pivotal to appreciating the power of recursion.

Implementing this recursively in a programming language is remarkably concise. A function would take the number of disks and the names of the source, destination, and auxiliary rods as parameters. It would recursively call itself to move smaller substacks, then move the largest disk, and then recursively call itself again to move the remaining substack. The elegance and efficiency of this recursive solution make the Tower of Hanoi a classic example of recursive problem-solving. Furthermore, the solution's inherent simplicity belies its profound recursive nature, revealing how complex problems can be broken down into manageable, repeatable units.

One might initially struggle with visualizing the recursive calls. It's helpful to trace the execution flow, perhaps even drawing diagrams showing the disk movements at each recursive step. You'll observe the pattern emerge, demonstrating how the recursive function progressively dismantles the problem into smaller, easier-to-manage subproblems. The key is to focus on the self-similarity and identify the base case that halts the recursion. This allows the function to successfully complete the task, moving all the disks from the source rod to the destination rod according to the rules.

The recursive approach to the Tower of Hanoi isn't just an elegant solution; it's also the most efficient way to solve the problem. Iterative solutions exist, but they often involve more complex bookkeeping and are less intuitive to understand. The recursive solution directly reflects the problem's inherent structure, making it easier to grasp and implement. The clear delineation of the base case and the recursive step is a hallmark of good recursive design, a concept that extends far beyond this particular puzzle. In essence, the Tower of Hanoi serves as a practical, engaging introduction to the power and elegance of recursive thinking. Understanding this puzzle provides a solid foundation for tackling more complex recursive algorithms. This example shows why recursion is more than just a programming technique; it's a powerful way of thinking about problems.

3 Recursive Data Structures

Linked lists, at their core, exemplify recursive structures. Each node points to the next, forming a chain. Consider traversing a linked list to find a specific value. You start at the head; if the value is found, you're done. If not, you recursively call the same function on the rest of the list (the list starting at the next node). This elegant simplicity highlights recursion's power in handling inherently self-similar data structures. The base case, crucial in preventing infinite recursion, is encountering either the desired value or the end of the list (a null pointer). Understanding this fundamental recursive approach to list traversal unlocks further operations like insertion, deletion, and searching. Mastering this foundational concept significantly improves understanding for more intricate data structures. The recursive nature is clearly visible, each step mirroring the structure.

Trees, another prominent example, present a more complex yet equally recursive nature. A tree comprises nodes, each potentially having child nodes. This hierarchical structure itself defines recursion. Imagine a binary tree, each node containing a value and two children – a left and a right subtree. Functions such as tree traversal (preorder, inorder, postorder) easily map to recursive algorithms. Preorder traversal, for instance, visits the current node, then recursively traverses the left subtree, and finally the right. Similarly, inorder traversal mirrors the recursive structure, proceeding through the left subtree, visiting the current node, and finally traversing the right subtree. The elegance of this recursive strategy allows for

effective, concise code, although iterative approaches are also possible.
Graphs, unlike trees, don't possess the same rigid hierarchical structure. However, their recursive nature becomes apparent when considering graph traversal algorithms. Depth-first search (DFS), a popular graph traversal technique, embodies recursion. It starts at a given node, explores as far as possible along each branch before backtracking. The recursive implementation elegantly mirrors this exploration: visit the current node, then recursively call DFS on each unvisited neighbor. The base case is simple: if there are no unvisited neighbors, the recursion stops. Understanding the recursive approach to graph traversal simplifies the complexities, making intricate navigation algorithms more understandable. It's important to note that while breadth-first search exists, it's often more naturally implemented iteratively.
Binary search trees (BSTs) elegantly combine the ordered nature of sorted data with the recursive structure of trees. Each node in a BST holds a key (value) and has at most two children: left and right. The key in the left subtree is always less than the parent's key, while the key in the right subtree is always greater. This ordering property is vital in efficient searching. A recursive search algorithm mirrors the BST structure: if the target key matches the current node's key, the search succeeds; otherwise, the search recursively continues on the left or right subtree, depending on the key's value, again based on the fundamental characteristic of the tree.
Binary heaps, a type of tree-based data structure, also have a strong recursive foundation. A binary heap is a complete binary tree that satisfies the heap property: either the value of each node is greater than or equal to the value of its children (max-heap) or less than or equal to (min-heap). The recursive nature manifests most prominently in heap operations like insertion and deletion. Insertion, for instance, requires recursively adjusting the heap structure to maintain the heap property after adding a new node. This might involve repeatedly comparing and swapping nodes to main-

tain the heap property following insertion. Similarly, deletion (typically of the root node) necessitates recursively rearranging elements to restore the heap's balanced structure and preserve the heap property. The recursive approach often simplifies implementation while providing efficient ways to manage the binary heap structure.

3.1 Linked Lists

Linked lists, at their core, are a fundamental data structure characterized by a sequence of nodes, each containing data and a pointer to the next node in the chain. The elegance of this structure lies in its simplicity and the natural recursive relationship between each node and the rest of the list. This recursive nature makes them ideal for exploring recursive algorithms. Consider the simple act of traversing a linked list: you start at the head, examine the data, and then recursively traverse the rest of the list (which is itself a linked list starting at the next node). This self-referential property perfectly embodies the essence of recursion.

Unlike arrays, which offer direct access to elements through indexing, linked lists require traversal from the head to access a specific node. This sequential access might seem inefficient compared to arrays, but it grants significant flexibility. Insertion and deletion of nodes are remarkably straightforward; you merely adjust a few pointers, a far simpler operation than shifting array elements. This efficiency advantage in modifying the list structure is crucial in scenarios where frequent insertions or deletions are necessary. Imagine a dynamic system needing constant updates; a linked list's flexibility shines here, allowing for efficient modification without the overhead of array restructuring.

Let's consider a recursive function for summing the values within a linked list. The function, sumList, would take the head of the list as input. If the list is empty (the base case), the sum is zero. Otherwise, it adds the value of the current node to the recursive call of sumList applied to the rest of the list (which is the list starting from the next node). This beautifully illustrates the breakdown of a complex task – summing the entire list – into smaller, identical subtasks – summing sub-lists. The recursive calls continue until the base case is reached, at which point the accumulated sums are returned level by level up the call stack, ultimately yielding the sum of the entire list.

Implementing this recursive function requires careful attention to the base case and the recursive step. The base case, as mentioned, is the empty list; this prevents infinite recursion. The recursive step involves adding the current node's value to the sum obtained from recursively processing the remaining part of the list. The code must accurately manage the pointers to move down the list during each recursive call and then correctly aggregate the results back up. Testing thoroughly, with different list sizes and value arrangements, is crucial to ensure the function's correctness. Edge cases, such as an empty list or a single-node list, must be explicitly considered and handled appropriately to prevent unexpected errors.

Beyond summing, many other list operations lend themselves beautifully to recursive solutions. Searching for a specific value, for example, can be implemented recursively: Check if the current node's value matches the target. If it does, you're done. If not, recursively search the rest of the list. The recursive approach might appear less efficient than an iterative approach for simple list operations like searching in certain situations due to the function call overhead. However, the elegance and clarity of recursive solutions often outweigh the performance difference, particularly for more complex list manipulations. Furthermore, certain recursive operations, like reversing a linked list, might have inherent complexities that make a recursive solution more intuitive and easier to understand and debug. Consider the relative simplicity and readability of a recursive reversal compared to an iterative approach; such improvements in code clarity can be more valuable than minor performance gains in many development contexts.

The recursive nature of linked lists extends beyond basic operations. More advanced tasks, such as merging two sorted linked lists, can also benefit from a recursive approach. The function would recursively compare the heads of the two lists, selecting the smaller value and adding it to the merged list, and then recursively merging the remaining portions. This process efficiently combines the sorted lists without explicitly iterating through every element. The recursive structure mirrors the divide-and-conquer paradigm, a powerful algorithmic strategy often seen in more advanced algorithms and data structures. A recursive solution to merging, while perhaps slightly less space-efficient than an iterative approach in some cases, frequently offers a significant increase in code clarity and maintainability.

Mastering linked lists and their recursive implementations provides a strong foundation for understanding more intricate data structures such as trees and graphs. The principles of recursive traversal and manipulation directly apply, making the transition smoother. Understanding the recursive nature of these structures is critical for their effective utilization in problem-solving. By grasping this concept, you are well-equipped to handle the complexities of more challenging recursive data structures. The investment in understanding the recursive intricacies of linked lists pays dividends when tackling advanced concepts later in your studies. Therefore, take your time, experiment with different code examples, and fully grasp the power and elegance of recursive approaches within linked lists before moving on. This solid base will significantly ease your journey through subsequent chapters.

3.2 Trees

Trees are hierarchical data structures, fundamentally recursive in nature. Each node, except for the root, has precisely one parent, mirroring the self-similar structure central to recursive thinking. Understanding this recursive definition is crucial to effectively implementing and manipulating tree-based algorithms. We can visualize a tree as a collection of nodes connected by edges, forming a parent-child relationship that extends downwards from a single root node. This structure naturally lends itself to recursive solutions because any subtree within the main tree is also a tree, possessing the same fundamental properties.

Consider a simple binary tree, where each node has at most two children – a left child and a right child. Implementing operations like tree traversal (inorder, preorder, postorder) becomes incredibly elegant using recursion. For instance, inorder traversal involves recursively visiting the left subtree, processing the current node, and then recursively visiting the right subtree. The elegance stems from the inherent self-similarity of the task; traversing a subtree is identical to traversing the entire tree—a classic recursive pattern.

Beyond simple binary trees, more complex structures like general trees or n-ary trees (where a node can have more than two children) also benefit from recursive solutions. These trees frequently model real-world hierarchical data, such as file systems (where directories are nodes and files are leaves), organizational charts (where employees are nodes and reporting relationships define the connections), and abstract syntax trees (ASTs) in compiler design (representing program structure). In each case, the recursive nature of the structure simplifies implementation and understanding of complex manipulations.

Recursive functions for tree manipulation often follow a standardized pattern. A base case, usually representing an empty tree or a single node, stops the recursion. The recursive step breaks the problem down into smaller subproblems involving the children nodes, recursively calling the function on these subtrees. The results from the subproblems are then combined to produce the result for the entire tree. This divide-and-conquer approach is fundamental to efficient tree algorithms.

Furthermore, when implementing recursive algorithms for tree manipulation, efficiency is paramount. Uncontrolled recursion can easily lead to stack overflow errors, especially with deeply nested trees. Strategies such as tail recursion (where the recursive call is the last operation in the function) can help prevent this, depending on compiler optimization capabilities. Additionally, employing iterative solutions instead of recursion might be more efficient in specific scenarios, particularly with very large trees where the overhead of recursive function calls becomes significant.

However, remember that recursion is not always the optimal solution. Iterative approaches, while possibly more verbose, can offer performance advantages in specific cases, especially when dealing with extremely large trees or performance-critical applications. The choice between a recursive and iterative solution often depends on factors such as the specific operation, the size of the tree, and the available hardware resources. Consider the trade-offs before selecting a methodology. Profiling your code and measuring its performance can help determine the best approach for a given application.

Efficient tree traversal algorithms, for example, heavily rely on proper handling of the recursive structure. Depth-first search and, to a lesser extent, breadth-first search can be elegantly implemented recursively, making use of the implicit tree structure to navigate through the nodes. These methods underpin many essential algorithms in graph theory, artificial intelligence (search algorithms like A*), and compiler design (syntax tree analysis). Careful consideration of space and time complexity is essential when designing recursive tree algorithms, especially for large datasets where the recursive depth can be substantial.

In conclusion, trees, as inherently recursive data structures, are highly amenable to recursive algorithms. Their self-similar properties make them ideal candidates for elegant and concise solutions to various computational problems. However, careful consideration of efficiency and the potential for stack overflow errors is crucial to creating robust and performant implementations. The choice between a recursive or iterative approach is often context-dependent, and a thorough analysis of the specific problem and its constraints should guide the selection process. Remember to always consider the trade-offs and to optimize your solutions for the specific task at hand. Mastering recursive techniques for tree manipulation is a cornerstone skill in computer science, enabling the efficient and elegant solution of diverse and challenging problems.

3.3 Graphs

Graphs, unlike the linear structures we've encountered, represent relationships between data points. Imagine a social network; each person is a node, and the connections between them, friendships, are the edges. This simple analogy captures the essence of a graph: a collection of nodes (or vertices) and edges connecting them. The edges can be directed (like a one-way street) or undirected (like a two-way street), leading to different graph types with unique properties and application scenarios. Understanding these fundamental differences is crucial for choosing the appropriate algorithms and data structures for efficient graph manipulation. We'll explore various graph representations and common algorithms that leverage recursion effectively.

Recursive algorithms find a natural home in graph traversal, particularly depth-first search (DFS). DFS, as the name suggests, systematically explores a graph by going as deep as possible along each branch before backtracking. Imagine you're exploring a maze: you'd follow one path as far as it goes, hitting dead ends, then retrace your steps to explore other paths. DFS mirrors this process, using recursion to track its progress. Each node visited marks the beginning of a recursive call, exploring its neighbors recursively until a base case is reached—either reaching a target node or exhausting all connected paths from that point. The recursive calls create a call stack that implicitly keeps track of the path taken. Returning from a recursive call indicates backtracking, allowing DFS to explore other branches.

A contrasting approach, breadth-first search (BFS), typically doesn't employ recursion directly. Though it's possible, it's less intuitive. BFS explores a graph level by level. Think of it like searching a tree: you'd start at the root, then check all its children, followed by their children, and so on. In contrast to DFS's depth-first exploration, BFS maintains a queue of nodes to visit, ensuring that nodes closer to the starting point are explored first. BFS is often implemented iteratively using queues, though recursive implementations are possible. The choice between DFS and BFS depends on the specific problem; DFS is often favored for finding paths, while BFS excels in finding the shortest path in unweighted graphs.

Representing graphs in a computer program requires careful consideration. The two most common approaches are adjacency matrices and adjacency lists. Adjacency matrices are essentially two-dimensional arrays where each element (i, j) indicates whether an edge exists between node i and node j. This approach provides fast access to check for the existence of an edge but can be inefficient for sparse graphs, consuming significant memory for graphs with many nodes and few edges. Sparse graphs, those where the number of edges is significantly smaller than the square of the number of nodes, are frequently encountered in real-world applications. In such cases, adjacency lists offer a more space-efficient representation.

Adjacency lists represent a graph as a collection of lists, one for each node. Each list contains the nodes directly connected to that node. This approach is particularly efficient for sparse graphs, as it only stores the existing edges, avoiding the wasted space of an adjacency matrix in representing non-existent connections. While adjacency matrices offer constant-time edge checking, adjacency lists' performance depends on the list implementation; with linked lists or similar data structures, finding an edge becomes O(N) time complexity, where N is the number of nodes. However, the space savings makes it preferable for sparse graphs. The choice between adjacency matrices and adjacency lists depends on the graph's density and the algorithm's requirements. Understanding the trade-offs between time and space complexity is crucial for optimizing the graph implementation for the given problem.

Beyond basic traversal, recursive algorithms play a key role in many graph algorithms, such as topological sorting, which orders nodes in a directed acyclic graph (DAG) such that for every directed edge from node A to node B, node A appears before node B in the ordering. This is crucial in tasks involving dependencies, such as build processes or scheduling tasks. Finding strongly connected components in a directed graph, identifying sets of nodes where every node is reachable from every other node within the set, also frequently uses recursive techniques. These advanced applications highlight the versatility of recursion in solving complex graph problems. Mastering recursive techniques is, therefore, essential for tackling the range of challenges posed by graph data structures and algorithms. The efficient handling of these structures opens up new opportunities for solving complex problems across various domains, from network analysis to software engineering.

3.4 Binary Search Trees

Binary search trees, or BSTs, are a fundamental data structure perfectly suited for demonstrating the power of recursion. Their hierarchical nature, with each node branching into smaller subtrees, mirrors the recursive decomposition of problems. Understanding this inherent recursive structure unlocks efficient algorithms for searching, inserting, and deleting nodes.

Crucially, the definition of a BST itself is recursive: a BST is either empty, or it contains a root node with a value, a left subtree containing only nodes with smaller values, and a right subtree containing only nodes with larger values. This elegant self-similarity forms the bedrock of recursive operations within the BST.

Let's explore a common operation: searching for a specific value. A naive, iterative approach would require traversing the entire tree in the worst case. However, a recursive search elegantly exploits the BST's structure. The search function checks the root node's value. If the target value matches, it returns true. If the target value is smaller, it recursively calls itself on the left subtree; otherwise, it recursively calls itself on the right subtree. This approach prunes large sections of the tree with each recursive call, leading to significantly improved efficiency, especially for balanced trees. The base case for this recursion is reaching an empty subtree, indicating the absence of the target value.

Insertion follows a similar recursive pattern. To insert a new node, the algorithm recursively traverses the tree, guided by the value of the new node. It ultimately identifies the appropriate location to insert the new node as a leaf, effectively expanding the tree while maintaining the BST property. The recursive calls continue until an empty subtree is found – the insertion point.

Deletion, however, is more complex. It requires careful consideration of various scenarios: deleting a leaf node, a node with one child, or a node with two children. While recursion can still be effectively applied, the implementation will necessitate more intricate logic to handle these cases. Deleting a node with two children typically involves finding its in-order successor (the smallest node in the right subtree) or predecessor (the largest node in the left subtree), replacing the deleted node's value with that of its successor/predecessor, and then recursively deleting the successor/predecessor from its original location. This ensures the BST property is maintained throughout the deletion process.

The recursive nature of BST operations contributes to their conceptual el-

egance. However, uncontrolled recursion can lead to stack overflow errors if the tree is extremely deep or unbalanced. For very large or heavily skewed trees, an iterative approach might prove more efficient in practice. But for most applications involving moderate-sized BSTs, the elegance and simplicity of recursive solutions often outweigh any minor performance considerations. The recursive approach fosters a cleaner, more readable, and arguably more intuitive codebase compared to its iterative counterparts. The inherent recursive structure of the data structure aligns beautifully with the recursive implementation of its operations, resulting in a very natural and efficient way to handle the underlying data.
Furthermore, understanding how to implement these recursive operations on BSTs is crucial for grasping more complex recursive algorithms. BSTs provide a relatively straightforward context for learning about the process of designing, implementing, and debugging recursive functions, which builds a strong foundation for tackling more intricate problems involving recursive data structures and algorithms later on. The conceptual clarity gained from working with BSTs forms a stepping stone to tackling more challenging algorithms. The principles learned here directly apply to understanding other recursive data structures, like trees and graphs, and lay the groundwork for more complex problems. Mastering BSTs therefore allows you to directly progress in your understanding of recursion and its diverse applications. Many advanced data structures and algorithms build upon the foundational principles of BSTs. So learning this structure is an essential step in your broader study of computer science.

3.5 Binary Heaps

A binary heap, unlike a binary search tree, doesn't maintain any specific ordering between parent and child nodes regarding their values. Instead, it's defined by its heap property: in a min-heap (the type we'll focus on), every parent node's value is less than or equal to the values of its children.

This property ensures the minimum element is always at the root, making it incredibly efficient for priority queue implementations. Imagine it like a tournament bracket; the winner (smallest value) always bubbles to the top. This structure is inherently recursive; each subtree is itself a min-heap.

The recursive nature is apparent in the heapify operation, a crucial component for building and maintaining the heap property. Heapify takes a node and its subtree as input. It recursively checks if the node violates the min-heap property. If a child node has a smaller value, they swap positions. This process continues recursively down the subtree until the min-heap property is restored throughout that section. Visualize a small ripple effect; the swap triggers a potential violation further down, repeating until stability is achieved.

Building a heap from an unsorted array leverages this recursive heapify function. We start from the last non-leaf node and work our way up. For each node, we call heapify to ensure its subtree satisfies the min-heap property. Consider it a bottom-up construction; the leaves are inherently heaps (trivially satisfying the property), and we iteratively 'heapify' the upper levels to integrate them consistently. This process effectively organizes the entire array into a min-heap.

Extracting the minimum element is straightforward – it's the root node. The challenge lies in maintaining the heap property after removal. We replace the root with the last element in the heap, effectively removing the minimum. Now, the heap property is likely violated at the root. To rectify this, we initiate heapify at the root node, initiating a recursive process to restore the min-heap structure throughout. Think of it as repairing a small breach; the adjustment at the top may cause ripples below, requiring further adjustments.

Insertion into a binary heap also involves maintaining the heap property. After adding a new element to the end of the underlying array, we recursively 'bubble up' this new element. This involves comparing the element with its parent and swapping if necessary. This continues until the element finds its appropriate position, upholding the min-heap structure. The recursive 'bubble up' essentially seeks the correct location for the newcomer within the already organized structure, ensuring the entire heap stays a cohesive unit.

The practical applications of binary heaps are extensive. Priority queues, fundamental in many algorithms, rely on binary heaps to efficiently manage elements ranked by priority. They are used in algorithms like Dijkstra's shortest path algorithm, where finding the node with the shortest tentative distance is paramount. The heap's constant time complexity for both finding the minimum and extracting it allows for rapid selection of the most suitable candidate in each iteration.

Furthermore, binary heaps are crucial in heapsort, a comparison-based sorting algorithm. Heapsort constructs a heap from the input array and then repeatedly extracts the minimum element, placing it in its sorted position. This process continues until all elements are sorted. The efficiency stems from the heap's inherent structure, which allows for quick identification and removal of the next smallest element. The recursive nature of heapify underpins this algorithm's effectiveness, guaranteeing each step maintains the integrity of the heap structure.

Implementing binary heaps in code usually requires careful handling of array indices to represent the parent-child relationships. For instance, the parent of a node at index i is generally located at (i-1)/2 (integer division). Children reside at 2i+1 and 2i+2. These relationships are integral to the recursive operations we've discussed, allowing efficient navigation through the heap structure and minimizing unnecessary operations. The direct mapping between array indices and tree nodes is pivotal for the recursive implementation, turning theoretical operations into concrete executable code.

Understanding binary heaps transcends mere data structure comprehension. It opens doors to understanding the power of recursive thinking in algorithm design. The beauty of the binary heap lies not just in its efficient performance but also in the elegant recursive algorithms that underpin its operations. Mastering its intricacies strengthens your ability to design and analyze efficient algorithms for a wide range of applications. It shows how a seemingly simple structure can provide the backbone for complex algorithms and efficient solutions to real-world problems. This fundamental understanding will serve as a crucial building block for tackling more advanced recursive data structures and algorithms in your programming journey. The efficient manipulation of the heap, enabled by the recursive nature of its algorithms, underpins its wide applicability in various computer science domains.

4 Advanced Recursion

Divide and conquer algorithms elegantly tackle complex problems by recursively breaking them into smaller, more manageable subproblems. Imagine sorting a massive deck of cards. Instead of comparing every single card to every other card, a divide and conquer approach would first split the deck in half, then sort each half recursively, finally merging the two sorted halves. This significantly reduces the overall comparisons needed, leading to a much faster sorting time—O(n log n) compared to the $O(n^2)$ of a naive approach. The key is identifying a way to divide the problem into independent subproblems, solve them recursively, and then effectively combine their solutions to obtain the final result. This methodology is widely applicable in numerous computational tasks, proving its power and efficiency. Mastering this technique significantly enhances a programmer's problem-solving abilities.

Dynamic programming provides a powerful optimization strategy for recursive algorithms that often involve overlapping subproblems. Consider the Fibonacci sequence calculation: each number is the sum of the two preceding ones. A naive recursive implementation recalculates the same Fibonacci numbers multiple times. Dynamic programming elegantly solves this redundancy. Instead of repeatedly computing the same values, it stores the results of subproblems in a table or array (often called a memoization table). When the algorithm encounters a subproblem it's already solved, it simply retrieves the stored result from the table, avoiding redundant computations. This dramatically reduces the runtime complexity, transforming exponential time algorithms into polynomial time, a significant improvement for large input sizes. This optimization is particularly crucial when dealing with computationally expensive recursive functions. Let's consider a practical example: finding the shortest path between two points in a graph. A naive recursive approach might explore all possible paths, leading to an exponential time complexity. However, a dynamic programming approach can significantly improve this. By storing the shortest path lengths to intermediate nodes, the algorithm avoids recalculating these distances repeatedly. It cleverly uses this stored information to construct the overall shortest path, effectively pruning the search space and reducing computational time. This illustrates the practical advantage of dynamic programming in optimizing recursive solutions for problems involving interconnected subproblems, showcasing its efficiency and importance in enhancing the performance of recursive algorithms.

Beyond these core techniques, several crucial aspects need careful consideration when implementing advanced recursive algorithms. One critical element is the base case. The base case forms the foundation of any recursive algorithm, defining the condition under which the recursion stops. Without a correctly defined base case, your algorithm might enter an infinite loop, consuming unbounded resources and ultimately crashing. Therefore, meticulously crafting the base case is paramount. It's the cornerstone that prevents an uncontrolled cascade of recursive calls, ensuring the algorithm terminates correctly and efficiently. Careful consideration and testing of the base case are essential before moving to complex algorithms.

Another critical point lies in the management of the call stack. Each recursive call adds a new frame to the call stack, consuming memory. Deeply nested recursive calls can lead to stack overflow errors, a common pitfall in recursive programming. One can mitigate this by employing techniques like tail recursion optimization (when the recursive call is the last operation in the function) or iteratively implementing the algorithm if possible. These techniques reduce the stack usage, enhancing the robustness of the recursive implementation and prevent the dreaded stack overflow errors, which are often challenging to debug. Preventing these errors is a crucial aspect of creating robust recursive algorithms. Efficient memory management is crucial in writing effective and dependable recursive code.

Finally, carefully analyzing the time and space complexity of recursive algorithms is essential. Understanding how the algorithm's resource usage scales with the input size is critical for predicting its performance and identifying potential bottlenecks. Using techniques like Big O notation helps you formally express this complexity, enabling you to compare different approaches and choose the most efficient solution. Thorough complexity analysis guides you in making informed design choices, improving algorithm efficiency and optimizing performance, a fundamental aspect of software engineering. Therefore, understanding time and space complexity is essential for any programmer aiming to develop high-performance recursive solutions.

4.1 Divide and Conquer

Imagine you're faced with a massive jigsaw puzzle—thousands of pieces, a chaotic jumble. Trying to solve it all at once seems daunting, bordering on impossible. Divide and conquer offers a solution: break the puzzle into smaller, manageable sections. Solve each section independently, then combine the completed sections to form the final picture. This fundamental strategy, applicable far beyond puzzles, lies at the heart of many efficient algorithms. It's a recursive approach, cleverly breaking a large problem into smaller, self-similar subproblems.

The power of divide and conquer stems from its ability to simplify complexity. By recursively breaking down a problem, we reduce the size of each subproblem, until we reach a trivial base case easily solvable. This base case, like a single, easily identifiable piece in our jigsaw puzzle analogy, provides a solid foundation upon which to build the overall solution. The solutions to these smaller subproblems are then combined, often in a straightforward manner, to construct the solution to the original, larger problem. This stepwise refinement significantly reduces the overall complexity of the task.

Consider the classic Merge Sort algorithm. This algorithm elegantly exemplifies the divide-and-conquer principle. It starts by dividing an unsorted list into smaller sublists until each sublist contains only one element (our base case: a single element list is inherently sorted). Then, it repeatedly merges these sorted sublists to produce larger sorted sublists. The process continues until a single sorted list encompassing all elements is obtained. The elegance of the approach lies in its simplicity; the merging process itself is a relatively straightforward operation, yet the combined effect is a highly efficient sorting algorithm with a time complexity of O(n log n).

Another striking application is found in the realm of binary search. When searching for a specific element within a sorted array, a divide-and-conquer approach can drastically reduce the search time. Instead of linearly scanning the entire array, the algorithm repeatedly divides the search space in half. It compares the target element with the middle element of the current search space. If they match, the search ends successfully. If the target element is smaller, the search continues in the lower half; if larger, it focuses on the upper half. This recursive halving continues until the element is found or the search space is exhausted. The result is a significantly faster search algorithm with a time complexity of O(log n), a dramatic improvement over the linear O(n) complexity of a brute-force search.

However, while divide and conquer provides powerful tools, it's crucial to understand its limitations. The overhead of recursively dividing the problem can sometimes negate the benefits of solving smaller subproblems.

If the subproblems are not significantly smaller than the original problem, the recursive calls can lead to increased computational costs. Furthermore, the process of combining the solutions of the subproblems can become complex and computationally expensive depending on the nature of the problem. Careful consideration of these factors is vital to ensure that the divide-and-conquer strategy yields an efficient solution. In some cases, a different algorithmic approach might prove more efficient.
The choice of a divide-and-conquer approach isn't always straightforward. We must carefully assess the problem at hand. Does it naturally lend itself to being broken down into smaller, self-similar subproblems? Is the cost of dividing and combining the solutions less than the cost of solving the original problem directly? A keen eye for recognizing the inherent recursive structure of a problem is fundamental. Understanding how to effectively divide the problem and efficiently combine the solutions requires careful analysis and thoughtful design. Mastering this skill opens doors to crafting elegant and efficient solutions for a vast range of complex problems. The power of "divide and conquer" lies not only in its algorithmic elegance, but also in its intuitive appeal—a reflection of how we often tackle challenges in our daily lives, breaking them into smaller, more manageable tasks.

4.2 Dynamic Programming

Dynamic programming is a powerful optimization technique that transforms inefficient recursive algorithms into highly efficient ones. It achieves this by cleverly storing and reusing the results of subproblems, avoiding redundant computations. Imagine calculating the nth Fibonacci number recursively; you'd recalculate many values repeatedly. Dynamic programming eliminates this redundancy.
Instead of repeatedly computing the same subproblems, dynamic programming tackles them systematically, storing their solutions in a table

or other data structure. When a subproblem is encountered again, the algorithm simply retrieves the stored result, significantly speeding up the process. This method is particularly beneficial for problems exhibiting overlapping subproblems, where the same smaller problems appear multiple times within the larger problem's recursive structure.

Consider the classic example of finding the shortest path in a graph. A naive recursive approach might explore many paths repeatedly, leading to exponential time complexity. Dynamic programming, however, would store the shortest distance from a starting node to each other node. Once a shortest distance is computed, it's saved, and subsequent calculations use this pre-computed value, drastically reducing the computation time.

There are two primary approaches to dynamic programming: top-down (memoization) and bottom-up (tabulation). Memoization is essentially a straightforward enhancement of a recursive solution. We modify the recursive function to check if a result for a given input already exists; if so, it's returned directly; otherwise, the computation proceeds, and the result is stored for future use. This approach maintains the elegance of recursion while gaining the efficiency of dynamic programming.

Tabulation, on the other hand, takes a more iterative approach. It builds a table of solutions from the bottom up, starting with the smallest subproblems and progressively working towards the final solution. This avoids the overhead of recursive function calls, often leading to slightly faster execution. The choice between memoization and tabulation often depends on the specific problem and the programmer's preference; both approaches share the same fundamental goal of eliminating redundant computations.

Implementing dynamic programming requires careful consideration of the problem's structure. You need to identify the overlapping subproblems and define a suitable data structure (often a table or array) to store the results. The structure of this table directly reflects the way you break down the larger problem into smaller, self-similar subproblems. Correctly defining this structure is crucial for the algorithm's success. For instance, in the case of the Fibonacci sequence, the table naturally maps index to Fibonacci number.

Furthermore, the order in which you process the subproblems matters. In tabulation, you must process them in an order that guarantees the availability of previously calculated solutions when needed. Incorrect ordering can lead to incorrect results. This is less of a concern with memoization because it only calculates the needed values. However, memoization requires a bit more overhead with recursive calls.

Let's consider a practical application: the 0/1 knapsack problem. This classic optimization problem involves selecting items with maximum value from a set of items with weight constraints. A recursive solution would explore all possible subsets of items, leading to exponential time complexity. A dynamic programming approach, however, builds a table storing the maximum value achievable for each weight capacity from 0 to the maximum weight allowed. This table is populated iteratively, efficiently determining the optimal solution.

Choosing between recursion and dynamic programming isn't always straightforward. Pure recursion is often easier to understand and implement initially, but it can be vastly less efficient for problems with overlapping subproblems. Dynamic programming provides a path to significantly improve performance, but it requires a more structured approach to problem-solving, careful design of the table, and proper ordering of subproblem solutions. Understanding both methodologies and their tradeoffs is essential for crafting efficient algorithms. The choice ultimately depends on the nature of the problem and the desired balance between code readability and performance optimization.

5 Recursion in Practice

Merge sort elegantly demonstrates the power of recursion in sorting. It recursively divides the unsorted list into halves, sorts each half recursively, and then merges the sorted halves. This divide-and-conquer strategy ensures efficiency, with a time complexity of O(n log n), significantly faster than simpler O(n^2) algorithms for large datasets. Understanding how this recursive splitting and merging works is key to grasping its efficiency. The base case, a list with one or zero elements (already sorted), stops the recursion; otherwise, the process continues until every element finds its rightful place.

Unlike merge sort's elegance, quicksort's recursive approach is a bit more chaotic. It chooses a pivot element and partitions the array around it, placing all smaller elements before it and all larger elements after. This partitioning step itself is recursive, applied to the sub-arrays on either side of the pivot. While the average-case time complexity is also O(n log n), a poorly chosen pivot can lead to worst-case O(n^2) performance, highlighting the importance of pivot selection strategies in practical quicksort implementations. The choice of pivot greatly influences the algorithm's performance, making it a more nuanced example of recursive problem solving compared to the predictable behavior of merge sort.

Tree traversal algorithms are natural fits for recursion. Consider preorder, inorder, and postorder traversal of a binary tree. Each method systematically visits every node, utilizing recursion to explore the left and right subtrees. Preorder visits the root, then the left subtree, then the right; inorder visits the left subtree, then the root, then the right; and postorder traverses the left subtree, the right subtree, and finally the root. The recursive nature neatly mirrors the hierarchical structure of the tree, making the implementation concise and intuitive. Understanding the differences between these traversals provides a fundamental understanding of tree manipulation, essential in many applications such as efficient database indexing systems and XML processing.

Graph algorithms, such as depth-first search (DFS), also benefit significantly from a recursive approach. DFS explores a graph by starting at a node, visiting all its unvisited neighbors recursively, and then backtracking to explore other branches. This recursive exploration ensures that all connected nodes are visited. While breadth-first search (BFS) is often implemented iteratively, it can also be written recursively, although it's less common, as the iterative approach better handles the queue-like structure of the algorithm. DFS, however, lends itself naturally to the recursive paradigm and offers a simpler and often more efficient way to systematically traverse a graph's interconnected nodes.

Implementing recursive algorithms effectively often requires careful consideration of memory management. Deep recursion can lead to stack overflow errors if the recursive calls go too deep, exceeding the available stack space. Techniques like tail recursion optimization, where the recursive call is the very last operation performed, can help mitigate this risk, as some compilers can optimize tail-recursive functions into iterative loops, avoiding excessive stack usage. Understanding these limitations and employing optimization strategies is crucial for writing robust and efficient recursive programs, preventing unexpected crashes and ensuring reliable performance even in complex scenarios. Therefore, careful code design is essential.

Understanding these practical applications of recursion—from sorting and tree traversal to graph algorithms—is vital for any programmer. Mastering these techniques empowers you to tackle complex problems efficiently and elegantly. This chapter has only scratched the surface; the versatility of recursion extends far beyond these examples. By combining recursive thinking with an understanding of optimization strategies and potential pitfalls, you can unlock its power and create efficient, powerful solutions for a wide range of programming challenges. Remember to always consider the base case and carefully plan your recursive calls to avoid infinite loops. The elegance and power of recursion can transform complicated problems into simple, manageable pieces. Mastering recursion opens many possibilities to the serious programmer. The efficiency of recursive algorithms is often apparent when dealing with tree-like or hierarchical data structures. Furthermore, the clarity and conciseness of recursive code makes it a valuable addition to any programmer's toolkit. Recursive techniques are integral to writing efficient and elegant algorithms.

5.1 Sorting Algorithms

Sorting algorithms, fundamental to computer science, often benefit from recursive approaches. Merge sort, for instance, elegantly divides an unsorted list into smaller sublists until each contains only one element (the base case). These single-element lists are inherently sorted. The algorithm then recursively merges these sorted sublists, combining them into larger sorted sequences until the entire list is ordered. This divide-and-conquer strategy leads to a guaranteed O(n log n) time complexity, regardless of the input data's initial arrangement, making it highly efficient even for large datasets. Understanding the recursive calls and the merging step is key to grasping its power. Think of it like recursively organizing a messy filing cabinet—you break it down into smaller drawers, organize each drawer individually, and then combine the organized drawers back into one perfectly ordered cabinet. The elegance and efficiency of this recursive approach are undeniable.

Quicksort, another prominent recursive sorting algorithm, operates differently. It selects a 'pivot' element from the list and partitions the remaining elements into two sublists: those less than the pivot and those greater. This partitioning happens recursively, applied to each sublist until all sublists have only one element. This method, while also possessing an average-case time complexity of O(n log n), can degrade to O(n^2) in the worst-case scenario—typically when the pivot selection consistently leads to highly unbalanced partitions. Careful pivot selection strategies, such as choosing a random pivot or the median-of-three, are crucial in mitigating this worst-case behavior and maintaining the algorithm's efficiency in practice. You might visualize this as a recursive process of separating a bag of mixed candies into piles based on color, then further dividing each pile until each contains only one candy of a single color. The speed of this method depends largely on your initial candy separation strategy.

The recursive nature of these algorithms isn't merely an implementation detail; it's intrinsically linked to their effectiveness. The elegance lies in how naturally they break down a large problem into smaller, self-similar subproblems. This decomposition, combined with the base case handling (single-element lists for both Merge Sort and Quicksort), guarantees termination and yields efficient solutions. Furthermore, the recursive structure often translates into concise and readable code, despite the algorithm's complexity. However, understanding the recursive calls and the associated space complexity is vital. Each recursive call adds a new frame to the call stack, potentially leading to stack overflow errors for extremely large input lists. Therefore, while recursion provides an elegant and often efficient way to implement sorting algorithms, programmers must always be mindful of these limitations, using iterative versions when dealing with exceptionally large datasets or resource-constrained environments.

Recursion provides an elegant and powerful approach to designing and implementing sorting algorithms. Merge sort, with its consistent O(n log n) time complexity, offers a reliable and efficient solution. Quicksort, though susceptible to worst-case $O(n^2)$ performance, delivers high average-case efficiency, making it a popular choice. However, careful consideration of pivot selection and potential stack overflow issues is critical for its practical application. Mastering recursive sorting techniques involves not only understanding the algorithm's logic but also appreciating its inherent elegance and the practical considerations needed for efficient and robust implementation, allowing you to harness its power while avoiding common pitfalls. The choice between merge sort and quicksort often depends on specific application requirements and the expected characteristics of the input data. For instance, if guaranteed O(n log n) performance is paramount, merge sort may be preferred; however, if average-case efficiency is acceptable and the worst-case scenario is less likely, quicksort might prove more efficient. Understanding both approaches is crucial for a well-rounded understanding of recursive algorithm design and its application in practical sorting problems. A programmer's toolkit must include a thorough grasp of the recursive approach to sorting algorithms, allowing for both elegant solutions and efficient implementations in various contexts.

5.2 Tree Traversal

Trees, fundamental data structures in computer science, are naturally recursive. Their hierarchical structure, where each node can have child nodes that are themselves trees, perfectly mirrors the recursive definition of a function calling itself. Understanding this inherent recursion is crucial for efficient tree traversal. We'll explore three common methods: preorder, inorder, and postorder traversal.

Preorder traversal follows a "root-left-right" approach. Imagine you're meticulously exploring a sprawling family tree; you'd first visit the root (the ancestor), then delve into the left branch, exploring all its descendants before moving to the right branch and repeating the process for each subtree. In code, this translates to visiting the current node, recursively traversing its left subtree, and then its right subtree. This method is particularly useful when you need to create a copy of the tree, or to serialize it into a linear structure such as a list or string. The resulting output reflects the hierarchical structure directly, with the root node coming first.

Inorder traversal is the "left-root-right" method. Think of it as systematically cataloging books in a library: you'd start at the far left of the shelves (the left subtree), meticulously recording each book's information before moving to the central section and then to the right. This recursive approach ensures that nodes are processed in a sorted order if the tree is a Binary Search Tree (BST). This is extremely beneficial when dealing with data that needs to be ordered. Imagine creating an index or a sorted list from the data within the tree, the inorder traversal would create the index directly.

Postorder traversal is the "left-right-root" technique. This method is analogous to dismantling a complex object: you'd completely disassemble the smaller components (left and right subtrees) before finally removing the main assembly (the root). This ordering proves beneficial in tasks such as calculating the size or height of a tree, or deallocating memory associated with the nodes of a tree. This process guarantees that the subtrees are completely processed before their parent node is visited, crucial for maintaining a consistent state within the data structure. This order is less intuitive but very useful for certain calculations done on trees.

The implementation of these traversals relies heavily on recursion. Each method utilizes a recursive function that calls itself on the left and right subtrees. A crucial element in each function is the base case: when the current node is null, the recursion stops. Without this base case, the function would call itself infinitely, resulting in a stack overflow error, a common issue when dealing with recursive algorithms. Therefore, meticulously defining this base case is vital for preventing this type of error.

Understanding these traversal methods is critical for many tree-based algorithms. They form the backbone of various operations, from searching and sorting to efficient data manipulation. While iterative approaches exist, the recursive solutions often provide a cleaner, more intuitive, and more easily understandable implementation, especially for beginners grappling with the concepts of recursion and tree structures. Mastering these traversal techniques provides a strong foundation for tackling more complex tree algorithms and further enhances one's understanding of recursive programming. The beauty of recursion lies in its ability to elegantly handle complex hierarchical structures like trees, making intricate operations surprisingly simple to code and understand. Furthermore, understanding the nuance between these different approaches and the contexts in which they excel is a vital step in becoming proficient in tree-based algorithm development. Proficiency in tree traversal is not just a technical skill; it's a key to unlocking a deeper understanding of recursion itself.

5.3 Graph Algorithms

Graph algorithms frequently leverage recursion's inherent ability to explore interconnected data. Consider depth-first search (DFS), a classic example. DFS systematically explores a graph's nodes by going as deep as possible along each branch before backtracking. Imagine traversing a maze; DFS is akin to following a single path until you hit a dead end, then returning to a previous junction and trying another route. The recursive implementation naturally mirrors this exploration process. A recursive function visits a node, marks it as visited, and then recursively calls itself for each unvisited neighbor. The base case is reached when there are no more unvisited neighbors. This simple, elegant structure showcases recursion's power in tackling complex graph problems. The recursive nature leads to a concise and understandable code, even for moderately large graphs.

Conversely, breadth-first search (BFS), while often implemented iteratively, can be implemented recursively as well, though perhaps less efficiently. BFS explores a graph level by level, visiting all neighbors at the current level before moving to the next. While not as immediately intuitive as DFS's recursive implementation, BFS can still be achieved through a recursive approach using a queue-like structure. The recursive function would process nodes level by level. Each recursive call would process one level of the graph, and it would terminate once all levels have been explored. This technique requires careful management of the queue to ensure proper ordering, demonstrating the trade-offs between different algorithmic approaches. The iterative approach often proves more efficient due to the overhead of recursive function calls.

Understanding these contrasting approaches highlights the versatility of recursion. While iterative solutions might offer performance advantages in certain cases, recursive solutions often provide greater clarity and ease of implementation, particularly in scenarios where the inherent structure of the problem lends itself to a self-similar, recursive decomposition, such as many graph traversal problems. For instance, finding the shortest path between two nodes in a graph often utilizes algorithms like Dijkstra's algorithm, which can be implemented either recursively or iteratively. The recursive variant usually involves recursively exploring all possible paths from a starting node, keeping track of the shortest path discovered so far. The recursive calls explore different branches of the graph systematically. Each call evaluates the path length, updating the shortest path if a shorter one is discovered, highlighting the recursive logic in problem-solving.

Beyond basic traversal, more complex graph algorithms also benefit from recursive techniques. For instance, finding strongly connected components in a directed graph can effectively use recursion. This algorithm identifies sets of nodes where each node is reachable from every other node within the set. A recursive approach involves exploring the graph by performing DFS to discover the components. The recursion elegantly handles the traversal and identification of these components. The algorithm's recursive nature allows for a clean and efficient implementation, as the recursive calls naturally explore the interconnectedness of the nodes. It's crucial to handle the backtracking and ensure accurate identification of the components through proper management of the recursive calls.

Furthermore, topological sorting, crucial for tasks like scheduling and dependency resolution, often utilizes recursive techniques in its implementation, though iterative approaches exist. Topological sorting arranges nodes in a directed acyclic graph (DAG) such that for every directed edge from node A to node B, node A appears before node B in the ordering. A recursive approach would involve recursively processing nodes, ensuring that all prerequisites are processed before a node itself is added to the sorted list. However, caution must be exercised to prevent infinite recursion in case of cycles, making this problem more challenging than many traversal algorithms. Detecting and handling cycles becomes an important consideration in the design of a recursive solution to this. The function needs to be designed to detect such cycles and handle them appropriately, perhaps by raising an exception or using a different strategy for those parts of the graph.

In conclusion, while iterative approaches may sometimes provide optimization benefits, especially for breadth-first search, the recursive nature of many graph algorithms offers significant advantages in terms of clarity, conciseness, and elegant implementation. Mastering recursive techniques unlocks a powerful toolset for tackling complex graph problems, especially those involving intricate explorations of graph structures. The inherent recursive structure of many graph problems naturally leads to efficient and concise recursive solutions. Choosing between recursive and iterative solutions often involves considering factors like performance and readability, and the nature of the problem being solved significantly influences the best approach to adopt.

6 Optimization and Efficiency

Memoization is a powerful technique for optimizing recursive functions. Imagine calculating the Fibonacci sequence recursively without it—each call to fibonacci(n) recalculates fibonacci(n-1) and fibonacci(n-2) repeatedly. This leads to exponential time complexity. Memoization elegantly solves this by storing the results of previous function calls. When the function is called again with the same input, the stored result is immediately returned, avoiding redundant computations. This dramatically reduces execution time, transforming an exponential algorithm into a linear one. Implementing memoization often involves using a dictionary or a similar data structure to store the (input, output) pairs. The key is the function's input, and the value is the corresponding output. Before performing a recursive call, the function checks the dictionary; if the input exists, it uses the stored value; otherwise, it proceeds with the recursive computation, storing the result in the dictionary afterward. This simple addition can significantly enhance the performance of many recursive algorithms. Consider the classic example of calculating Fibonacci numbers; with memoization, the time complexity drops from O(2n) to O(n).

Tail recursion is a special form of recursion where the recursive call is the very last operation performed in the function. This characteristic is crucial because it allows compilers and interpreters to optimize the function's execution. In a tail-recursive function, the recursive call doesn't need to be added to the call stack; instead, the current stack frame can be reused, preventing stack overflow errors for very deep recursion levels. Not all programming languages support tail call optimization; however, for those that do, it's a valuable optimization strategy. To convert a recursive function to tail-recursive form, you often need to use an accumulator variable that accumulates the results of the recursive calls. The accumulator is passed as an argument to each recursive call, and the final result is returned when the base case is reached. For instance, consider the factorial function. A standard recursive implementation might involve recursively multiplying the current number by the factorial of the number minus one. A tail-recursive version, however, would involve an accumulator initialized to 1 and accumulating the product in each call until it reaches the base case. This transformation ensures the recursive call is the final operation. The benefits of tail recursion are evident when dealing with deeply recursive algorithms where stack overflow is a serious concern.

Stack overflow is a common error encountered in recursive programming, particularly when dealing with very deep recursion or functions with large stack frames. It occurs when the program attempts to allocate more stack space than is available. The stack is a crucial area of memory used to manage function calls, storing local variables, return addresses, and other relevant information. In recursive functions, each recursive call adds a new frame to the stack. If the recursion is excessively deep—for example, processing a very large data structure recursively or dealing with a recursive function lacking a proper base case—the stack can quickly overflow, causing the program to crash. Preventing stack overflow is critical for writing robust recursive code. One strategy is to carefully design the base cases of your recursive functions to ensure they are reached efficiently. Another crucial aspect is to consider the use of iterative algorithms as an alternative, particularly in situations where deep recursion is anticipated. Iterative approaches tend to have smaller memory footprints and are less prone to stack overflow. Finally, consider techniques like tail recursion optimization, which, as mentioned earlier, can effectively prevent stack overflow by reusing the current stack frame instead of adding new ones. Optimizing the recursive algorithm itself can also help; minimizing unnecessary operations or using more efficient data structures can reduce the depth of the recursion. Understanding the limitations of the stack is essential in writing efficient and stable recursive programs.

6.1 Memoization

Imagine calculating the nth Fibonacci number. A naive recursive approach, while elegant, suffers from repeated calculations of the same Fibonacci numbers. You recalculate fib(3) multiple times when computing fib(5), leading to exponential time complexity. This is inefficient, especially for larger values of 'n'. Memoization offers a solution to this problem of redundant computation; it's a powerful optimization technique.

Memoization essentially involves storing the results of expensive function calls and returning the cached result when the same inputs occur again. Think of it as a lookup table for your function's outputs. When your recursive function encounters a previously computed value, it fetches the stored result instead of recomputing it. This dramatically improves performance, particularly for recursive functions with overlapping subproblems, a hallmark of many recursive algorithms, such as Fibonacci sequence calculation or dynamic programming problems.

Let's consider a practical example. We'll implement a memoized version of the Fibonacci sequence calculation in Python. We'll use a dictionary to store the computed Fibonacci numbers; the key will be the input 'n', and the value will be the corresponding Fibonacci number. Initially, the dictionary is empty. As the recursive function encounters Fibonacci numbers, it stores them in the dictionary. When it encounters a subsequent call with the same input, it retrieves the pre-computed value directly from the dictionary. This straightforward approach prevents redundant calculations

and significantly reduces the runtime.
The implementation is quite simple. We define a function that first checks if the input 'n' is present as a key in our memoization dictionary. If it is, the stored value is immediately returned. Otherwise, the standard recursive calculation is performed, and the result is stored in the dictionary before being returned. This ensures that future calls with the same input will directly access the cached result. The function's base cases remain unchanged – fib(0) and fib(1) are handled as usual. The time complexity of this memoized version improves dramatically from exponential to linear, making it much more efficient for larger values of n.
This technique is particularly useful in scenarios with high computational costs associated with repeated calls involving the same inputs. This is true for many recursive problems. Consider the scenario where the computation of a function involves complex mathematical operations, database queries, or network requests. Memoization significantly reduces the number of times these expensive operations are performed, leading to substantial performance improvements. The memory trade-off, however, must be acknowledged. Storing previously computed results requires additional memory, a factor to consider, especially when dealing with a vast number of possible input values.
The advantage of memoization isn't limited to just recursive functions; it can be effectively used to optimize iterative functions as well. Any function with repeated computations involving the same inputs is a candidate for memoization. In fact, the concept of memoization underpins the principles of dynamic programming, a powerful algorithmic technique heavily reliant on storing and reusing previously computed results to solve optimization problems efficiently. Dynamic programming often employs memoization, but it often handles the storage and retrieval of results systematically, frequently using tables or arrays. Yet, the fundamental idea remains the same: avoid repeated calculations.

When designing recursive algorithms, it's essential to assess whether memoization could enhance efficiency. If the algorithm involves many recalculations of the same values, memoization might be the key to substantial performance improvement. It's a simple but effective technique to improve the performance of computationally expensive tasks. Remember that the decision to use memoization should be based on a careful analysis of the time and space complexity trade-offs. It's not a universal solution; the additional memory usage must be considered, and its benefit is most significant when repeated computations are costly. In summary, memoization is a practical and vital optimization technique, especially relevant when dealing with recursive functions, and it is worthy of your attention as you develop and refine your recursive algorithms.

6.2 Tail Recursion

Tail recursion represents a specific form of recursion where the recursive call is the very last operation performed within the function. This seemingly minor detail holds significant implications for optimization and efficiency. Unlike standard recursive calls, where the function needs to remember its previous state for subsequent steps, a tail-recursive function doesn't require this additional memory. The compiler or interpreter can optimize tail-recursive calls by transforming them into iterative loops, effectively eliminating the overhead associated with function call stacks. This optimization dramatically reduces the risk of stack overflow errors, a common problem in deeply nested recursive functions. Imagine calculating the sum of a list of numbers recursively; a non-tail-recursive approach would stack each call until the base case is hit, adding memory pressure. A tail-recursive version, however, can be rewritten efficiently without this stack buildup, providing a significant performance benefit. The key is structuring your code so the recursive call is the final action—no further computation is pending after the recursive call returns. This allows for the optimized transformation, making tail recursion a valuable tool for programmers tackling computationally intensive problems.

The benefit of this optimization is substantial, especially when dealing with large datasets or complex recursive algorithms. Stack overflow errors, which occur when the call stack exceeds its allocated memory, become significantly less likely with tail recursion. This stability allows for tackling problems previously intractable due to memory limitations. For instance, consider a recursive function that processes a large tree structure. A non-tail-recursive implementation would risk a stack overflow, whereas a tail-recursive version could process even deeply nested trees efficiently. This robust memory management opens up opportunities for solving a wider range of recursive problems. The practical implications extend beyond avoiding errors; the performance increase can be substantial, especially in scenarios involving numerous recursive calls.

However, it's crucial to understand that not all programming languages or compilers support tail call optimization. Some languages might simply not perform the optimization, and others might have specific requirements for the code structure to be recognized as tail-recursive. In such cases, the performance benefits might not be realized. It's vital to check the language documentation and compiler settings to ascertain whether tail call optimization is available and how to write code that takes advantage of it. Some languages actively encourage tail recursion; understanding this aspect is crucial for efficient programming. Even with optimization, poorly written recursive functions, whether tail-recursive or not, can still be inefficient. Careful algorithm design and attention to base cases remain paramount.

Therefore, the decision of whether to employ tail recursion should be a strategic one, informed by both language capabilities and algorithmic considerations. If your language supports tail call optimization and your algorithm is amenable to a tail-recursive formulation, the benefits of enhanced

efficiency and reduced risk of stack overflow are clear. However, if your language lacks this support or your algorithm fundamentally doesn't lend itself to tail-recursive implementation, forcing it could lead to more complex and less readable code without tangible performance improvements. The primary goal should always be writing clear, correct, and efficient code. Tail recursion can be a powerful tool to achieve these goals, but it's not a silver bullet applicable to every recursive problem. Understanding the nuances of its implementation and limitations is crucial for effective use. Proper understanding is therefore critical.
Let's consider a concrete example. Imagine you're building a function to reverse a linked list. A standard recursive approach might involve recursively reversing the rest of the list and then appending the current node to the end. This is not tail-recursive because the append operation happens after the recursive call. A tail-recursive version, however, would involve passing the already reversed portion of the list as an argument to the recursive call. The recursive call would then be the last operation. This subtle shift in how the function is structured allows for compiler optimization, leading to significantly improved performance, especially for lengthy lists. Analyzing the structure of your recursive functions and identifying opportunities to structure them as tail-recursive calls can substantially enhance the efficiency and robustness of your code, illustrating the powerful effect of careful algorithm design and implementation details. The key lies in recognizing when and how this optimization technique is most beneficial, and not merely resorting to it as a default optimization for every recursive function. This nuanced approach is vital for leveraging the advantages of tail recursion while avoiding potential pitfalls.

6.3 Avoiding Stack Overflow

The most dreaded error in recursive programming, the dreaded "stack overflow," stems from exceeding the program's call stack capacity. Imagine a stack of plates; each function call adds a plate. Too many calls, too many plates, and the stack collapses. This isn't about memory exhaustion in a general sense; it's specifically about the limited space reserved for function call information. Understanding this is crucial.

A recursive function, by its nature, generates multiple function calls, each consuming stack space. If the recursion goes too deep—for example, a poorly designed recursive function handling an excessively large input—the stack overflows, terminating your program abruptly. This isn't a graceful exit; it's a crash. The error message is usually quite clear, stating the exact problem: stack overflow.

So, how do you avoid this? First, scrutinize your base case. The base case is the condition that stops the recursion. Without a properly defined and reachable base case, your function will call itself endlessly, leading directly to a stack overflow. Ensure your base case is logically sound and easily reached given the expected input size. Carefully review your termination condition to make sure it will be met under every possible valid scenario. Test with both small and large inputs to identify potential problems.

Next, consider the problem's nature. Some problems are inherently more suited to iterative solutions. If you're wrestling with a problem that lends itself better to loops than recursion, switching to an iterative approach might be the best solution. While recursion can be elegant and efficient for certain tasks, forcing it onto an unsuitable problem will often lead to stack overflow issues, especially with larger inputs. Don't be afraid to step back and analyze your chosen approach.

Beyond that, optimize your recursion. Efficient recursive algorithms minimize redundant calculations. Techniques like memoization, discussed in a previous chapter, can significantly reduce the depth of recursion and therefore the risk of stack overflow. Memoization stores the results of previous calculations, preventing redundant computations, thus shrinking the call stack. The trade-off is increased memory usage for faster execution, a balance you need to consider in your algorithms.

Tail recursion is another powerful optimization technique. In tail-recursive functions, the recursive call is the very last operation performed. This allows compilers or interpreters to optimize the function by reusing the current stack frame rather than creating a new one for each recursive call. This drastically reduces stack usage, thus mitigating stack overflow issues. However, not all programming languages support tail-call optimization; in those cases, using this optimization may have little impact. Understanding how your programming language or compiler handles recursion is essential for effective optimization.

Furthermore, analyze your data structures. The size of the data you process directly affects the depth of recursion. Consider the worst-case scenarios – what inputs would trigger the deepest possible recursion in your function? For instance, sorting a nearly-sorted list with a recursive algorithm might perform better than sorting a completely randomized one, since the recursive calls will be less numerous. If your data structures are inefficient or contain more data than is necessary, they can drastically impact how much work your recursive algorithm needs to do, directly contributing to stack overflow. Carefully consider the size and structure of your data when using recursion.

Finally, employ iterative techniques when appropriate. Not all problems need recursive solutions. Many problems can be solved efficiently using iterative methods, often using loops, and avoiding the risks associated with deep recursion entirely. If your program struggles with stack overflow and an iterative alternative exists, it is often a better solution. Iterative solutions can be easier to debug and more predictable in their memory usage compared to recursive solutions. Using iterations, while it may not always be as elegant, will help you avoid common problems faced in recursion. The balance between elegance and practicality is essential in software engineering. Sometimes, the straightforward approach is the most reliable.

Always analyze your requirements to determine the optimal solution for your problem; the trade-off between elegance and efficiency should always be carefully weighed.

7 Real-World Applications

Fractal generation provides a visually compelling demonstration of recursion's power. Imagine generating a simple snowflake: start with a straight line. Then, recursively replace the middle third of that line with two lines forming an equilateral triangle. Repeat this process on each of the new line segments, again and again. The result, after many iterations, is a breathtakingly complex and self-similar fractal pattern, showcasing how a simple recursive rule can lead to stunning visual complexity. This process mirrors many natural phenomena, from branching trees to coastline formations. We see how recursively defined functions can create incredibly intricate and beautiful designs, illustrating the elegance and power inherent in this approach. The depth of the recursion directly correlates to the detail and complexity of the final image; a deeper recursion leads to more intricate structures and a higher resolution. The beauty lies not only in the visual outcome but also in the elegant simplicity of the underlying algorithm.

Compiler design heavily relies on recursion for tasks such as parsing. A compiler takes human-readable code and translates it into machine-readable instructions. Crucially, the structure of many programming languages is inherently recursive; statements can be nested within other statements, creating a hierarchical structure. Recursive descent parsing efficiently handles this hierarchical structure. Imagine a grammar rule defining an arithmetic expression: an expression can be a number, or it can be an expression plus another expression. A recursive function can perfectly mirror this definition, processing the expression from the innermost parentheses outward, making it ideal for handling the nested nature of many programming language constructs. This recursive approach directly maps to the grammar's recursive definition, providing an efficient and elegant solution for a fundamental compiler task. Consider the complexity of modern programming languages, the ease with which a recursive parser navigates such complex structures is a testament to the power and effectiveness of recursion in this context. Efficient parsing is critical to compiler speed and overall efficiency, impacting the speed and performance of countless software applications.

Game development utilizes recursion for numerous aspects, including artificial intelligence and game mechanics. Consider a game featuring an AI-controlled opponent. The AI might employ a recursive minimax algorithm to make strategic decisions. Minimax recursively explores all possible game states, evaluating potential outcomes and choosing the move that maximizes the AI's chances of winning, while minimizing the player's. The algorithm's recursive nature allows it to consider a vast number of potential game outcomes, resulting in a more intelligent and challenging opponent. Beyond strategic decision-making, recursion finds application in game-world generation, procedural content generation, and even in rendering complex 3D graphics. The effectiveness of recursive AI algorithms in games often hinges on efficiently managing recursion's inherent computational costs, highlighting the need for optimization techniques discussed previously. Furthermore, the recursive design of game environments can greatly simplify their coding and maintainability while adding considerable depth and complexity to the player experience.

Pathfinding algorithms, critical to many games and simulations, often employ recursive techniques. A classic example is depth-first search (DFS), which recursively explores a graph, systematically visiting all connected nodes. Imagine a character in a video game navigating a maze; DFS can efficiently find a path to the destination. The recursive nature of DFS allows it to explore paths systematically, backtracking when a dead end is encountered. While iterative versions exist, the inherent recursive nature of DFS makes it a natural and intuitive approach to pathfinding. The algorithm's effectiveness depends on the structure of the search space, and techniques like heuristics can be integrated to improve efficiency. Recursive pathfinding algorithms are instrumental for numerous applications, from determining navigation routes in computer games to optimizing logistics in supply chain management, illustrating the widespread utility of recursive thinking in solving real-world problems. The efficiency of these algorithms is critical in various contexts, influencing performance and the responsiveness of numerous systems.

The applications we've examined demonstrate recursion's versatility. From generating intricate fractals to powering sophisticated AI algorithms, recursion provides elegant and efficient solutions across diverse computational domains. While its use often requires careful consideration of efficiency and potential pitfalls such as stack overflow, when appropriately applied, recursion stands as a powerful and indispensable tool in the programmer's arsenal. Its inherent elegance and close relationship to many natural processes makes it an ideal approach to a wide array of challenging programming tasks. Understanding and mastering recursion unlocks the ability to address complex problems with solutions that are both efficient and intellectually satisfying.

7.1 Fractal Generation

Fractals, those infinitely complex shapes built from simple repeating patterns, are a stunning testament to the power of recursion. Imagine a snowflake: its intricate design, a seemingly endless repetition of smaller and smaller, yet self-similar, branches. This very structure, this self-similarity across scales, is what makes them so captivating and perfectly lends itself to recursive generation. Understanding how to programmatically create these intricate designs provides a strong practical application of recursive principles learned throughout this book.

We'll focus on generating two well-known fractal examples: the Sierpinski triangle and the Mandelbrot set. The Sierpinski triangle's construction is delightfully simple, relying on a recursive function that repeatedly subdivides a triangle into smaller, similar triangles. Start with a filled-in equilateral triangle. Recursively, remove the central inverted triangle, leaving three smaller triangles. Repeat this process on each of those smaller triangles, and so on, ad infinitum. The resulting image is a complex pattern characterized by self-similarity—zoom in on any part, and you'll see a smaller version of the whole. This is where our recursive function comes in; it dictates how many levels of recursion (how many times we repeat the subdivision) we want to implement, directly controlling the complexity of the final image.

The Mandelbrot set, on the other hand, takes a slightly different approach. It's defined by a complex number equation. Each point in the complex plane is tested for membership in the set based on whether a related sequence of numbers remains bounded, meaning it doesn't grow infinitely large. This testing, determining whether a point falls within the Mandelbrot set's boundary, is where recursion shines. The iterative process, calculating the sequence, naturally lends itself to a recursive function. The depth of recursion determines how precisely the boundary of the Mandelbrot set is defined; more recursion means a more detailed image, revealing more of its intricate beauty. In effect, the recursive calls progressively refine the image based on the iterative process, revealing increasingly detailed complexity.

The code implementation for generating these fractals involves recursion in two key aspects. Firstly, recursive functions define the processes for drawing each element of the self-similar patterns. Secondly, the level of detail in the fractals is directly controlled by the number of times these recursive functions call themselves. A simple counter within the function tracks the current recursion level. Reaching a predefined maximum recursion depth signals the base case, stopping the recursive calls. Careful selection of this depth is crucial; it's a trade-off between image detail and computational cost. Too many levels may lead to slow rendering times or even stack overflow errors (remember our earlier discussions on this important topic!).

These illustrative examples aren't just about pretty pictures; they highlight a profound connection between mathematical concepts and programming. The simplicity of the underlying rules contrasted with the visual complexity of the result shows the remarkable power of iterative and recursive processes. Furthermore, understanding how these fractals are generated offers insight into broader principles of self-similarity and recursive algorithms that have implications far beyond the realm of computer graphics.

For practical application, consider implementing these fractal generators in a language such as Python, utilizing its strong graphics libraries. Python's clear syntax and extensive libraries make it an ideal choice for visualization, but concepts translate readily to other languages. Begin by defining your recursive functions, clearly specifying the base cases, and carefully controlling the recursion depth to avoid performance issues. Remember to properly handle exceptions and implement error-checking mechanisms.

Beyond the Sierpinski triangle and the Mandelbrot set, numerous other fractals can be generated using similar recursive techniques. Explore variations of these fundamental fractals, or delve into generating entirely new ones. Consider experimenting with different color palettes or adding interactive elements to your programs, allowing users to adjust parameters and explore the resulting visual changes in real time. This hands-on experimentation will significantly enhance your understanding of both fractal generation and the practical application of recursive programming. The possibilities are nearly limitless—each modification, each parameter adjustment, each newly explored fractal reveals a deeper understanding of recursion's surprising power and elegance. The beauty of fractals and the elegance of recursive algorithms, combined, create a stunning spectacle, illustrating the power and potential of recursive programming techniques explored throughout this book.

7.2 AI and Machine Learning

Many machine learning algorithms rely heavily on recursive structures and processes. Consider decision trees, a fundamental concept in classification and regression. A decision tree recursively partitions data based on features, creating a tree-like structure where each node represents a decision and each leaf node represents a classification or prediction. Building such a tree involves recursively splitting the data until a stopping criterion is met, demonstrating a clear application of recursive thinking in a critical machine learning area. The efficiency and accuracy of these trees depend greatly on how effectively the recursive partitioning is implemented. Poorly designed recursive calls can lead to overfitting, where the model performs well on training data but poorly on unseen data, highlighting the importance of understanding recursive optimization techniques discussed earlier in the book. This optimization is crucial; without careful consideration, a recursively generated decision tree could become unwieldy and computationally expensive, rendering the model inefficient or unusable. Therefore, understanding the trade-offs between accuracy, complexity, and computational cost is paramount when applying recursion to decision trees.

Recursive algorithms also play a significant role in reinforcement learning, a powerful technique for training agents to make optimal decisions in complex environments. For example, the algorithm used to navigate a maze can involve a recursive approach, exploring possible paths and backtracking when necessary. This recursive exploration process allows the agent to find optimal paths efficiently and effectively. While iterative approaches exist for solving similar problems, recursive methods often offer a more intuitive and elegant way to model the problem's inherent structure, particularly in scenarios with branching possibilities or a hierarchical relationship between decisions. This is particularly true when dealing with scenarios that involve uncertainties or stochastic processes – recursion handles the variability inherent in these situations naturally, creating a robust and versatile solution. This recursive approach becomes increasingly advantageous as the complexity of the environment increases, showcasing the power and scalability of recursive algorithms in tackling complex AI challenges.

Neural networks, another cornerstone of modern machine learning, often utilize recursive concepts in their architectures and training procedures. Backpropagation, the algorithm used to train many neural networks, involves recursively calculating gradients to update the network's weights and biases. This recursive computation process allows the network to learn from its errors and improve its performance over time. The mathematical operations behind backpropagation are inherently recursive, propagating error signals backward through the network layer by layer. Therefore, an understanding of recursive processes and their computational implications is crucial for grasping the fundamental mechanisms of neural network training and optimization. Effectively implementing backpropagation requires a keen awareness of computational efficiency to avoid excessive processing time or resource demands. Thus, the concepts of memoization and tail recursion, previously discussed, become especially important when considering the large-scale computation involved in neural

network training.
Furthermore, the use of recursive data structures in machine learning is ubiquitous. Many graph-based algorithms, fundamental to applications like recommendation systems and social network analysis, leverage the recursive nature of graph structures to traverse nodes and edges efficiently. Similarly, recursive structures are employed in the design of various AI systems, from decision trees and Bayesian networks to game-playing algorithms. Understanding how to implement and optimize recursion on these data structures is essential for designing efficient and scalable machine learning algorithms. Failure to consider the recursive nature of these structures can lead to inefficient algorithms that struggle with large datasets, highlighting the importance of careful consideration when designing solutions. Mastering recursive techniques not only improves algorithm efficiency but also provides a deeper understanding of how many machine learning models fundamentally operate.
In conclusion, recursion plays a multifaceted and vital role across a wide spectrum of machine learning algorithms and data structures. From the recursive partitioning of decision trees to the backpropagation algorithm in neural networks and the traversal of graph-based data structures, recursion acts as an underlying pillar supporting the functionality and performance of numerous key components in machine learning systems. Understanding and mastering the principles of recursion, as outlined in this book, provides a solid foundation for developing efficient, robust, and scalable solutions in the ever-evolving field of artificial intelligence. Therefore, a thorough grasp of the material presented herein is crucial for anyone seeking to contribute to or advance the fields of machine learning and AI. Mastering these recursive concepts equips you with the tools to build sophisticated and high-performing algorithms, taking your skills beyond basic programming into the realm of cutting-edge AI development.

7.3 Compiler Design

Compilers, the unsung heroes of the programming world, transform our human-readable code into machine-executable instructions. Understanding their design reveals a fascinating application of recursion. At its core, a compiler's task is to analyze and translate code, a process inherently recursive.

Consider the parsing phase. A compiler needs to break down a complex program into smaller, manageable syntactic units. This often involves recursive descent parsing, where a parser function calls itself to analyze nested structures like function calls or nested loops. Imagine a function definition; the compiler needs to recursively parse its parameters, its body, and any nested functions within. This hierarchical structure mirrors the recursive nature of the parsing algorithm itself. The process repeats until it reaches the simplest grammatical units, the leaves of the syntax tree. Each recursive call handles a smaller portion of the overall task, ultimately building a complete representation of the code's structure. This recursive breakdown simplifies complex parsing logic, making it manageable and easier to implement.

The compiler then moves to semantic analysis, verifying that the code adheres to the programming language's rules. This stage, too, frequently employs recursive techniques. For instance, type checking – ensuring that operations are performed on compatible data types – often requires traversing the syntax tree recursively. The compiler checks each node's type and then recursively checks the types of its children. This recursive traversal efficiently ensures the entire program's type correctness. Errors are identified early in the compilation process, thanks to the systematic, recursive exploration of the code's structure.

Code generation, the final stage, also benefits from recursion. The compiler translates the parsed and analyzed code into assembly language or machine code, creating instructions for the target processor. This translation process might involve recursively generating code for nested structures. Consider a nested loop; the compiler would recursively generate code for the inner loop for each iteration of the outer loop, ensuring the correct execution order. The recursive approach simplifies code generation, mirroring the nested structure of the program itself. Optimizations within the compiler, such as those related to loop unrolling or common subexpression elimination, can also be implemented recursively, taking advantage of the recursive structure of the intermediate representation of the program.

Efficient compiler design requires careful consideration of the base cases for these recursive functions, preventing infinite loops. The base cases, often representing the simplest syntactic units or the end of a recursive structure, are crucial for the correct termination of the recursive calls. Without them, the compiler could enter an endless loop, failing to complete its task. The base case could be an empty list in list processing or a null node in tree traversal, both commonly encountered scenarios in recursive compiler algorithms. The implementation is very important and is the key for avoiding errors. The programmer must ensure that every recursive call makes progress towards a base case, reducing the complexity of the problem with every call.

Moreover, the recursive functions used in compiler design are often not tail-recursive. Tail recursion offers efficiency benefits, but it is often not easily achievable in the complex task of compiler construction. Memory management is also crucial; deep recursion, if not handled efficiently, can lead to stack overflows. However, many compiler implementations handle this by using iterative strategies or sophisticated memory allocation techniques within the recursive functions.

The elegant efficiency of recursion in compiler design cannot be understated. The recursive approach allows for a concise and elegant implementation of complex algorithms, enhancing maintainability and reducing complexity. While some stages may be naturally iterative, the significant role of recursion in compiler design remains undeniable. It provides a powerful paradigm for handling the hierarchical nature of programming languages, resulting in efficient and effective code generation. The use of recursive algorithms in compiler design is a testament to the power and elegance of recursion in solving complex computational problems. Therefore, understanding recursion is critical for anyone aspiring to delve deeper into the intricacies of compiler development. The recursive nature of the problem mirrors the recursive solutions that elegantly solve it.

7.4 Game Development

Game development frequently leverages recursion's elegance and power, particularly in areas demanding complex, self-similar structures or processes. Consider the creation of procedurally generated levels. Imagine a dungeon crawler where each room's layout is recursively defined: a central chamber might branch into four smaller chambers, each of which could similarly branch, creating a sprawling, intricate, and unpredictable environment that feels organically complex, rather than painstakingly hand-crafted room by room. The recursive function, given a set of parameters defining the room's size, number of branches, and possible features, would create the layout, then recursively call itself for each branch, ensuring consistent style and complexity throughout the entire dungeon. This not only saves significant design time but also allows for near-infinite variability, making each playthrough feel unique.

Building complex game objects also benefits greatly from recursive design. Think of a tree in a landscape; its branches naturally follow a recursive pattern, with each branch splitting into smaller branches, until reaching tiny twigs. Modeling this accurately requires a recursive function, where each branch's generation depends on the parent branch, repeating until a predefined depth or size is reached. The program recursively generates and places branches, leaves, and other small details, producing a visually realistic and computationally efficient tree model compared to manually placing each and every individual branch and leaf. This method scales remarkably well, allowing for the creation of highly detailed environments without excessive memory consumption or development time.

Implementing artificial intelligence (AI) within games provides another compelling use for recursion. Consider pathfinding, a cornerstone of many games, particularly strategy and role-playing games. A recursive algorithm, like a depth-first search, can efficiently explore possible paths for a non-player character (NPC) or unit to move towards a target. The algorithm recursively explores every possible route, potentially making decisions based on the shortest distance to the target, or the most unobstructed path, based on the game's mechanics. In games involving exploration or puzzle-solving, this method allows for extremely intricate level design without sacrificing the NPC's ability to navigate effectively and realistically. Recursive backtracking algorithms can also be invaluable in game AI design, allowing for the exploration of different strategic options and the selection of the optimal path.

Game physics simulations can also incorporate recursive techniques, particularly for modeling complex interactions or behaviors. Consider a simulation of a ragdoll character, where different parts of the body interact realistically. This can be achieved with a recursive function that updates the position and rotation of each joint, taking into account the forces acting upon it and the positions and orientations of its connected joints. The algorithm recursively checks and updates all the joints in the chain, from the body to the fingertips, ensuring that every part reacts appropriately to external forces and interactions. The recursive nature ensures accurate modeling of complex physical interactions. This recursive method enhances realism and dramatically reduces development time compared to a more conventional iterative approach.

Finally, consider the recursive nature of many game mechanics themselves. A branching narrative structure in an adventure game, where player choices lead to different outcomes, can be elegantly represented by a recursive algorithm that explores every possible path from a decision point. The algorithm calls itself recursively for each possible choice, branching out into a tree of potential outcomes. The recursive function handles each decision point, generating the appropriate game state for each path and storing the game information for quick retrieval. This enables a massive amount of varied gameplay with reasonable computing resources by maintaining the game's consistency and complexity.

In conclusion, recursion's adaptability shines in the design of diverse game elements, from level generation and modeling complex objects to creating sophisticated AI and physics simulations. Its efficient handling of self-similar problems reduces development time and enhances game design complexity with natural and intuitive solutions. Mastering recursive techniques is a significant asset for any aspiring game developer.

7.5 Pathfinding Algorithms

Pathfinding algorithms are crucial in numerous applications, from video games guiding characters to navigation systems directing vehicles. These algorithms determine the optimal route between two points within a given environment, often represented as a graph where nodes represent locations and edges represent connections. Understanding the recursive nature of many pathfinding solutions is key to efficient implementation and comprehension. Consider a simple maze: finding a path is essentially exploring branches recursively until the exit is located.

One common recursive approach employs Depth-First Search (DFS). DFS explores a single branch as deeply as possible before backtracking and exploring other branches. Imagine yourself in a maze; you'd pick a path and follow it to its end. If it's a dead end, you retrace your steps and try a different path. This trial-and-error approach naturally maps to a recursive function: it checks a path, recursively calls itself to explore the next possible path from there, and ultimately returns either a successful path or null indicating no path exists. The recursive structure elegantly handles the backtracking required when a path leads to a dead end. The base case for this recursion is straightforward: if you reach the destination, the path is found, and you return the path; if you reach a dead end or have explored all possibilities, the function returns failure.

However, a naive implementation of DFS can be inefficient, particularly in large graphs. It might explore many fruitless paths before finding a solution, significantly increasing computation time. This is where optimized versions and alternative algorithms come into play. Algorithms like A* search, although often implemented iteratively, leverage heuristics (educated guesses) to prioritize paths more likely to lead to the destination. These heuristics are incorporated into a recursive approach to prioritize branch exploration, which dramatically reduces the search space, thus making it suitable for finding paths in complicated, complex and very large graphs. Consider it like having a map in the maze; you would choose paths that appear closer to the exit rather than blindly exploring all paths equally.

Furthermore, the representation of the environment plays a crucial role in pathfinding algorithm efficiency. Grid-based environments are relatively straightforward to implement with recursive approaches, using a simple system of coordinates to represent nodes and edges. However, more complex environments, such as those represented by weighted graphs, which require assigning costs to paths, may require modification of the recursive function to account for the path cost, which is a factor when finding the optimal solution. For example, in a road network, paths could be weighted by distance or traffic conditions.

The choice of the algorithm depends on the specific context. For simple environments, DFS might suffice. However, for more complex environments or real-time applications where efficiency is paramount, optimized algorithms such as A* search might be necessary. Recursive implementation adds a layer of elegance and can significantly simplify the logical structure, while an iterative approach might be more efficient in memory use if optimized correctly. Understanding both the recursive nature and the application of heuristics in more complex pathfinding algorithms is crucial to choosing and implementing a solution that balances computational cost with solution quality. Therefore, selecting a pathfinding algorithm is often a balance between the complexity of the environment and the time constraints of the application. This makes the understanding of many different approaches vital.

In conclusion, understanding pathfinding algorithms involves recognizing their recursive nature. While not all pathfinding techniques are inherently recursive, many utilize recursive principles such as depth-first exploration or recursive calls within optimized algorithm structures. Mastering this recursive perspective opens up new ways to approach these problems, facilitating efficient algorithm design and implementation. Remember that different approaches exist, and the optimal selection will often depend on the specific constraints of the application. Therefore, the choice of a pathfinding algorithm requires carefully considering the type of environment, the complexity of the problem, and the desired performance level. By understanding the trade-offs and employing suitable optimization techniques, you can create effective and efficient solutions for a wide range of pathfinding challenges. This deep understanding is essential for anyone working with graph algorithms and the wider world of algorithmic problem-solving. The versatility of recursive thinking allows for elegant solutions to a range of complex problems; mastering this approach is paramount to success in computer science.

www.ingramcontent.com/pod-product-compliance
Lightning Source LLC
LaVergne TN
LVHW022023200926
848481LV00007B/2513